Pot Luck

POT LUCK

MABLE HOFFMAN

with Jan Robertson

HPBOOKS

HPBooks
Published by The Berkley Publishing Group
A division of Penguin Putnam Inc.
375 Hudson Street
New York, New York 10014

Copyright © 2000 by Mable Hoffman
Book design by Richard Oriolo
Cover design by Jill Boltin
Cover art © by Katherine Edwards/StockArt.com

This book includes some recipes from Mable
Hoffman's *The Complete Tomato Cookbook*.

First edition: September 2000

Published simultaneously in Canada.

The Penguin Putnam Inc. World Wide Web site address is
http://www.penguinputnam.com

Library of Congress Cataloging-in-Publication Data

Hoffman, Mable, 1922–
    Pot luck / Mable Hoffman, with Jan Robertson—1st ed.
        p. cm.
    ISBN 1-55788-319-X
    1. Entrâés (Cookery) 2. Casserole cookery. I. Robertson, Jan.
II. Title.

TX740.H6155 2000
641.8—dc21
                                                00-033510

Printed in the United States of America

10 9 8 7 6 5 4 3 2 1

NOTICE: The recipes contained in this book are to be followed
exactly as written. Neither the publisher nor the author is responsible
for your specific health or allergy needs that may require medical
supervision, or for any adverse reactions to the recipes contained in
this book.

Contents

Introduction

One-dish meals are the keystones in every recipe collection. Reliable standards, they are repeatedly used for a wide range of options from entertaining to family dining.

In this collection you will also find main-dish salads for warm summer lunches and suppers, delightful brunch dishes that are perfect for leisurely weekend meals, and even sandwiches for when you want something just a little lighter. There are comfort foods that will provide a bit of nostalgia, family favorites, vegetarian entrees, and dishes that are special enough for company or an important family meal. Easy meals cooked in the slow cooker and that are just waiting for you to come home and enjoy them are also included. All the recipes take advantage of the offerings in a well-stocked supermarket, including many convenience products, and have been updated to fit today's lifestyles.

Casseroles and hearty soups and stews qualify as a meal-in-a-dish. They only need to be complemented by the addition of a crusty French roll and a fruit salad or a piece of garlic bread and a garden salad. If you are short on time, the salads and the garlic bread can be purchased at the supermarket on your way home. If you are entertaining or making a special meal, you might want to add a homemade dessert or one from your favorite bakery.

A complete one-dish meal is forgiving if dinner has to be postponed for a few minutes; it can stay warm in the oven, in the slow cooker, or in an electric skillet. This type of dish also makes a good choice to tote to pot lucks, a family picnic, or a tailgate party before the big game. The next time you ask, "What can I bring?" you will find several choices throughout this book, whether it's a vegetarian buffet or a special birthday celebration.

Ingredients

Use the best and freshest ingredients that are available. For better flavor, choose the grated Parmesan cheese in the deli or cheese counter rather than the canned kind on the shelf. Or purchase a block of Parmesan cheese, which keeps almost forever if well wrapped in the refrigerator, and freshly grate your own. Grate enough at one time for several meals; package in a tightly covered container and refrigerate. Freshly ground black pepper will give your creation the flavor it deserves. Vine-ripened tomatoes will always outshine the hard, pale tomatoes often available in supermarkets

With increasing interest in ethnic and regional cooking, grocers are stocking items unheard of a short time ago. Everything from fresh herbs to bottled condiments to exotic spices to new imported produce items are now available in supermarkets and make it possible to cook dishes from around the world without having to travel around town looking for the ingredients. Take advantage of this food bonanza. Travel to the Caribbean Islands one night by serving Beef, Black Bean, & Sweet Potato Casserole, page 103. Experience the spices of India while tasting Turkey Vindaloo, page 167. Expand your world and try something new.

In addition to the regional and ethnic ingredients, a wide range of new products are available that make cooking easier than ever before. These include refrigerated pasta and pizza crusts, various mixes, a variety of chicken and turkey products, precut vegetables and fruits, and prewashed salad mixes. Several already shredded cheeses make it easy to assemble a dish in minutes.

Stocking Up

Here are lists of some of the items that you might want to have on hand for last-minute meal preparation or unexpected guests. Anything fresh in the produce drawer is an added bonus that can be added to the foods listed below to make a complete meal without going shopping.

In the Cupboard

The following canned, bottled, and dried ingredients can be kept for several months. Use up old stock before buying new. Many cans are now dated so you can easily keep track of when they were purchased.

Artichoke hearts

Baking mix

Beans, canned and dried

Beef broth

Chicken broth

Corn

Couscous

Crabmeat

Dried herbs

Dried pasta, several shapes

Evaporated milk

Green chiles

Olives, ripe and green

Pasta sauces

Potatoes, canned and fresh

Rice

Salsas

Tomatoes

Tomato sauce

Tuna

In the Refrigerator

Don't let your refrigerator shelves become a home for "mystery food." Keep perishable foods well wrapped and use in a timely manner. Check "use-by" and "sell-by" dates when shopping.

Carrots

Celery

Cheeses, block and shredded

Dijon mustard

Eggs

Fresh pasta

Lemons and limes

Mayonnaise and salad dressing

Onions

Refrigerated piecrust

Refrigerated pizza crust

Sausages

Soy sauce

Steak sauce

In the Freezer

Items such as chicken breasts, fish fillets, and shrimp can be cooked while still frozen—a timesaver when you're in a hurry.

Boneless, skinless chicken breasts

Bread dough

Breads

Fish fillets

Lean ground beef or turkey

Nuts

Uncooked shrimp

Cookware and Small Appliances

When making one-dish meals it is helpful to have a selection of casseroles or baking dishes in different sizes, Dutch ovens or other large pots, a large regular or electric skillet, and a slow cooker. Oven-to-table cookware makes cleanup easier, because there are no serving dishes to wash. If you often take a dish to a social gathering, you might want one of the casserole dishes with its own insulated cover, designed to keep the contents warm during travel. Choose pans with nonstick surfaces whenever possible; the new surfaces are much improved. They last longer and make cleanup easier, because they are truly nonstick.

Slow Cookers

Slow cookers fit into the lifestyle of today's family. With everyone spending more time away from home, this method of cooking enables busy people to enjoy hot meals without having to resort to fast-food restaurants or take-out foods. The food is ready to eat when you return from shopping, school, or work. The food in a slow cooker does not need to be stirred (except for dried beans) or turned. Opening the lid to check on the dish just once means that the dish will need to cook for 15 to 20 minutes longer, because heat and steam escape when the lid is removed. The new slow cookers with the removable liners make cleanup easier.

Complete one-dish meals can be prepared in the slow cooker. To finish the meal, one family member could toss a green salad while another one sets the table—dinner is ready.

The slow cooker is also perfect for serving food on a buffet and for taking a hot dish to a pot-luck dinner. Even dishes cooked in a regular skillet or saucepan can be transferred to a slow cooker for travel and serving.

Electric Skillets

Electric skillets can be used to cook a dish and keep it warm for a short time without overcooking, because the temperature can be controlled. Nonstick surfaces make cleanup easy. Electric skillets are available in different sizes. Choose the one that best fits your needs.

Easy Weeknight Dinners

When a phone call to order a pizza seems to be the only solution to

dinner, think again. After a long day at work, turn to one of these

recipes for the answer. Smoky Sausage & Beef Pasta goes together

in a snap. Get a head start on Gingered Shrimp Skillet by

marinating and refrigerating shrimp in the morning and

completing it that evening. Or make Taste-of-the-Orient Omelet, a

quick-to-fix dish filled with fresh vegetables.

Baked Egg Rolls

Chicken & Orzo with Tropical Salsa

Fennel Turkey Toss

Gingered Shrimp Skillet

Hot German Potatoes & Knockwurst

Pacific Pesto Grilled Halibut

Quick Alfredo Noodle Bake

Smoky Sausage & Beef Pasta

Speedy Frittata

Taste-of-the-Orient Omelet

Turkey Polenta

Halibut with Fennel & Sun-Dried Tomatoes

Thai-Style Salmon

Tuscan-Style Turkey Special

Speedy Sausage Dinner

Macaroni with Sun-Dried Tomatoes & Goat Cheese

Turkey Tomato Sauté with Pasta

Baked Egg Rolls

MAKES 4 SERVINGS

These egg rolls are baked in the oven but they look steamed because they are not browned.

1 tablespoon vegetable oil

¾ pound boneless turkey breast, cut into 2 × ½-inch strips

2 tablespoons soy sauce

2 tablespoons cornstarch

1 cup chicken broth

1 to 2 baby bok choy, thinly sliced (about 2 cups)

1 (8-oz.) can sliced bamboo shoots, drained

2 green onions, sliced

4 mushrooms, sliced

8 (6 × 7-inch) egg roll wrappers

3 tablespoons hoisin sauce

Preheat oven to 350F (175C). Heat the oil in a 10-inch skillet over medium-high heat. Add the turkey; cook, stirring, until no longer pink, 2 or 3 minutes.

Combine the soy sauce, cornstarch, and broth in a small bowl; add to skillet. Cook, stirring, until slightly thickened and bubbly. Stir in the bok choy, bamboo shoots, onions, and mushrooms. Cook, stirring, until bok choy is softened, 1 to 2 minutes; cool slightly.

Place ½ cup of the turkey mixture diagonally along the center of an egg roll wrapper. Fold the bottom corner over the filling, then fold in the 2 corners. Starting at the bottom, roll up. Place, seam side down, in an 11 × 7-inch baking dish. Repeat with remaining turkey mixture and wrappers. Brush tops of rolls with hoisin sauce. Cover and bake 15 to 20 minutes, or until wrappers are cooked and filling is hot.

Chicken & Orzo with Tropical Salsa

MAKES 4 OR 5 SERVINGS

Quick chicken accented with a fruity island-inspired salsa.

1 tablespoon vegetable oil

1 pound boneless, skinless chicken breasts, cubed

1 clove garlic, minced

1 (8-oz.) jar or can prepared salsa (about 1 cup)

¾ cup chicken broth

1 medium red onion, chopped

¾ cup uncooked orzo pasta

TROPICAL SALSA

1 mango, peeled and chopped

1 avocado, peeled and chopped

2 tablespoons chopped fresh cilantro

Heat the oil in a large skillet over medium heat. Add the chicken and sauté, stirring occasionally, until brown on all sides. Stir in the garlic, prepared salsa, broth, red onion, and orzo. Cover and simmer about 12 minutes, or until the orzo is tender.

Meanwhile, make the Tropical Salsa: Combine the mango, avocado, and cilantro in a medium bowl.

Serve the chicken and orzo with the Tropical Salsa.

Fennel Turkey Toss

MAKES 4 SERVINGS

Using turkey sausage cuts the calories but not the flavor. Often used in Italian cooking, fennel has a slight anise or licorice flavor.

> 2 medium fennel bulbs with tops
>
> 1 tablespoon vegetable oil
>
> 1 small onion, chopped
>
> ¾ pound bulk sweet Italian turkey sausage
>
> 1 (15- to 16-oz.) can diced tomatoes, with juice
>
> 1 (8-oz.) can tomato sauce
>
> ½ teaspoon salt
>
> ⅛ teaspoon freshly ground black pepper
>
> 1 teaspoon dried Italian herbs
>
> 8 ounces uncooked wide egg noodles

Remove the top leaves from the fennel. Chop and set aside 1 tablespoon for garnish. Finely chop the fennel bulbs.

Heat the oil in large skillet over medium heat. Add the fennel and onion; cook, stirring, until fennel is softened, 5 to 10 minutes. Add the sausage; cook over medium heat, stirring to break up, until brown, 5 to 10 minutes. Add the tomatoes, tomato sauce, salt, pepper, and herbs. Simmer, covered, until the vegetables are tender and sauce has thickened, 20 minutes.

Meanwhile, cook the pasta according to package directions. Drain; serve the sauce over cooked pasta. Sprinkle with reserved fennel tops.

Gingered Shrimp Skillet

MAKES 4 SERVINGS

For a quick meal at the end of a busy day, marinate the shrimp in the morning and finish the recipe that evening.

3 tablespoons soy sauce

1 tablespoon ketchup

1 teaspoon grated fresh ginger

1 clove garlic, minced

¾ pound uncooked medium shrimp

1 cup uncooked long-grain white rice

1 tablespoon vegetable oil

1 yellow zucchini or pattypan squash, quartered and thinly sliced

1 yellow bell pepper, thinly sliced

3 tablespoons cornstarch

1 cup chicken broth

4 green onions, cut into 1-inch pieces

1 cup sugar snap peas

In a medium bowl, combine the soy sauce, ketchup, ginger, and garlic. Remove and discard the shells from the shrimp. Add the shrimp to the marinade; stir until well coated. Cover and refrigerate 2 or 3 hours or overnight.

Cook the rice according to package directions.

While the rice cooks, heat the oil in large skillet over medium-high heat. Drain the shrimp; reserve the marinade. Add the shrimp, squash, and bell pepper to the skillet. Stir-fry 3 to 4 minutes. Stir the cornstarch into the reserved marinade and stir into shrimp mixture with the broth, onions, and peas. Stir-fry over medium heat 2 to 3 minutes, or until slightly thickened and bubbly. Serve over rice.

Hot German Potatoes & Knockwurst

MAKES 4 SERVINGS

A flavorful sauce turns meat and potatoes into a satisfying meal.

4 to 5 large red-skinned potatoes

3 slices bacon, chopped

1 small onion, finely chopped

1 tablespoon all-purpose flour

1 tablespoon sugar

1 teaspoon dry mustard

½ teaspoon salt

½ teaspoon freshly ground black pepper

¼ cup white wine vinegar

½ cup beef broth

½ teaspoon celery seeds

4 knockwurst or bratwurst (about 12 ounces total)

2 tablespoons chopped fresh parsley

Cover the potatoes with water in a medium saucepan. Bring to boil; simmer until tender, 25 to 30 minutes. Drain, cool slightly, and cut into slices. Place the slices into a large heatproof bowl.

Fry the bacon in a medium saucepan over medium heat until almost crisp. Add the onion and cook until translucent, 5 to 10 minutes. Mix in the flour, sugar, mustard, salt, and pepper. Stir in the vinegar, broth, and celery seeds. Cook, stirring often, until thickened.

Meanwhile, heat the knockwurst according to package directions; cut each into 6 to 8 diagonal slices. Add the knockwurst to the potatoes. Pour the sauce over and toss to coat. Sprinkle with the parsley and serve warm.

Pacific Pesto Grilled Halibut

MAKES 4 OR 5 SERVINGS

A flavorful seafood dish, this is quick and easy to put together.

½ cup chopped fresh cilantro

1 clove garlic, minced

½ teaspoon freshly grated lime zest

1 tablespoon fresh lime juice

1 small jalapeño chile, seeded and chopped

1 tablespoon soy sauce

2 tablespoons vegetable oil

4 to 5 (about 1-inch-thick) halibut or swordfish steaks

2 (15-oz.) cans whole new potatoes, drained

Preheat broiler. In a food processor or blender, combine the cilantro, garlic, lime zest and juice, chile, and soy sauce. Blend until mixed. With processor or blender running, gradually pour in the oil and process until thickened.

Place the fish steaks on a greased broiler pan. Brush top of each steak with the sauce. Coat the potatoes with remaining sauce; place in broiler pan with the fish.

Broil about 10 minutes, or until fish flakes with a fork.

Quick Alfredo Noodle Bake

MAKES 4 SERVINGS

This recipe takes advantage of timesaving convenience foods. It can be ready for the oven in just a few minutes with no chopping or precooking.

1 (12-oz.) bag broccoli slaw mix (shredded broccoli, carrots, and red cabbage)

1 (6-oz.) package refrigerated grilled chicken breast strips

1 (17-oz.) jar alfredo pasta sauce

½ teaspoon crumbled dried basil leaves

3 cups crisp chow mein noodles

Preheat oven to 350F (175C). Grease a 9-inch-square baking dish.

In a large bowl, combine the broccoli slaw, chicken, alfredo sauce, and basil. Spread half of the mixture in prepared dish. Sprinkle with half of the noodles. Spoon remaining broccoli-chicken mixture over the noodles. Top with remaining noodles.

Bake 20 to 30 minutes, or until hot and bubbly.

Smoky Sausage & Beef Pasta

MAKES 4 SERVINGS

A handy recipe for a quick-and-easy dinner, the delicious smoky flavor comes from the sausage.

- ½ **pound lean ground beef**
- 1 **jalapeño chile, seeded and finely chopped**
- 4 **green onions, chopped**
- ½ **pound smoked sausage links, diced**
- 1 **teaspoon chili powder**
- 2 **(8-oz.) cans tomato sauce**
- 8 **ounces uncooked penne or macaroni**

Brown the ground beef in a large skillet over medium heat, stirring to break up. Stir in the chile, onions, and sausage. Cook, stirring, 5 minutes. Add the chili powder and tomato sauce. Simmer about 10 minutes to blend flavors.

Meanwhile, cook the pasta according to package directions; drain. Spoon the sauce over the pasta and toss to combine.

Speedy Frittata

MAKES 4 SERVINGS

Forget takeout. This Italian-style omelet takes just a few minutes to prepare and is packed full of flavor.

> 8 ounces hot Italian sausage (about 2)
>
> 1 small onion, sliced
>
> 1 medium zucchini, chopped
>
> 1 medium red bell pepper, chopped
>
> ½ cup chopped mushrooms
>
> 6 eggs
>
> ½ cup (2 ounces) shredded Cheddar cheese

Remove casing from the sausage; crumble into a 10- to 12-inch skillet. Cook over medium heat, stirring to break up, 2 or 3 minutes. Stir in the onion, zucchini, and bell pepper. Cook until the onion is softened, 5 to 10 minutes. Stir in the mushrooms.

Slightly beat the eggs in a medium bowl; pour over the mixture in the skillet. Sprinkle with the cheese. Lift edges to let uncooked eggs run under. Cook over medium-low heat until eggs are set, about 5 minutes. Cut into wedges.

Taste-of-the-Orient Omelet

MAKES 3 OR 4 SERVINGS

A wonderful solution for a late dinner or a special brunch, this omelet combines tastes of the Far East with jicama from Mexico.

½ **pound lean ground pork**

1 **small red bell pepper, cut into thin strips**

1 **medium carrot, peeled and cut into thin strips**

½ **teaspoon salt**

¼ **teaspoon freshly ground black pepper**

6 **eggs, beaten slightly**

2 **tablespoons hoisin sauce (see Note, below)**

½ **cup snow peas, cut into thin strips**

3 **green onions, cut into ½-inch diagonal slices**

½ **cup shredded jicama**

Soy sauce (optional)

In a large skillet over medium-high heat, cook the pork, bell pepper, and carrot until pork is no longer pink, 4 to 5 minutes. Sprinkle with the salt and pepper.

In a medium bowl, combine the eggs and hoisin sauce. Pour over the pork and vegetables. Sprinkle the pea pods and onions over the eggs. Lift edges to let uncooked eggs run under. Cover and cook over medium-low heat until eggs are set, 5 to 10 minutes. Top with jicama. Cut into 3 or 4 wedges. Serve with soy sauce, if desired.

NOTE

Hoisin sauce, a thick brownish Chinese sauce, is found with other Asian foods in the supermarket. Its sweet-spicy flavor makes it a good table condiment and a seasoning for cooking.

Turkey Polenta

MAKES 4 TO 6 SERVINGS

Leftover turkey is renewed by the addition of garden-fresh vegetables to make a soon-to-be-favorite dinner.

1 tablespoon butter or margarine

1 small onion, chopped

1 large poblano or other mild green chile, seeded and chopped

1 red or green jalapeño chile, seeded and chopped

Kernels from 2 ears of corn (about 1 cup)

4 cups chicken broth

1 ½ cups uncooked polenta or yellow cornmeal

1 ½ cups chopped cooked turkey

1 cup (4 ounces) shredded sharp Cheddar cheese

In a large saucepan, melt the butter over medium heat. Stir in the onion, chiles, and corn. Cook, stirring occasionally, until onions are softened, about 10 minutes. Remove from heat.

Add the broth, polenta, and turkey. Stir well. Bring to a boil over medium heat. Cook, stirring constantly, 8 to 10 minutes. Stir in the cheese until melted. Serve hot.

Halibut with Fennel & Sun-Dried Tomatoes

MAKES 4 SERVINGS

Cut off and save the delicate fresh fennel leaves to sprinkle on the finished dish.

- 1 tablespoon olive or vegetable oil
- 1 or 2 small fennel bulbs with tops, cut into 1 × ¼-inch matchstick pieces, leaves reserved
- 1 clove garlic, minced
- 1 tablespoon chopped chives
- 1 (16-oz.) jar thick salsa
- ⅓ cup sun-dried tomatoes in oil, drained and chopped
- ½ pound halibut or swordfish, cut into 1-inch pieces
- 1 cup uncooked long-grain white rice

Heat the oil in a large skillet over medium heat. Stir in the fennel and garlic. Cook, stirring occasionally, until fennel is almost tender, 10 to 15 minutes. Add the chives, salsa, tomatoes, and fish. Cook 5 to 10 minutes, or until fish flakes easily.

Meanwhile, cook the rice according to package directions. Spoon the tomato-fish mixture over the rice. Sprinkle with the reserved fennel leaves.

Thai-Style Salmon

MAKES 4 OR 5 SERVINGS

Lemongrass is a slender reedlike grass with a tart lemon flavor. It has a bulb-shaped base and a tough stalk. Just use the more tender part at the bottom.

1 small green serrano or jalapeño chile, seeded and chopped

2 tablespoons hoisin sauce

¼ cup fresh lemon juice

2 tablespoons light brown sugar

1 small stalk lemongrass, thinly sliced

1 clove garlic, minced

2 tablespoons chopped fresh cilantro

2 tablespoons vegetable oil

4 to 5 (about 1-inch-thick) salmon steaks

1 large bunch kale, coarsely sliced (about 6 cups)

Combine the chile, hoisin sauce, lemon juice, sugar, lemongrass, and garlic in a small saucepan. Heat over medium heat, stirring, until sugar dissolves. Remove from heat. Stir in the cilantro.

Heat 1 tablespoon of the oil in a large skillet over medium-high heat. Add the salmon. Spoon some of the chile mixture over salmon. Cook 5 minutes. Turn and cook until the fish flakes easily, 4 to 5 minutes. Remove salmon and keep warm.

Heat the remaining 1 tablespoon oil in skillet. Add the kale and cook just until leaves begin to wilt, about 5 minutes. Spoon onto individual plates. Top with salmon steaks and remaining sauce.

Tuscan-Style Turkey Special

MAKES 4 SERVINGS

Enjoy favorite Italian flavors from your own kitchen.

¾ ounce dried shiitake mushrooms

Hot water, for soaking

8 ounces uncooked linguine or fusilli pasta

¼ cup all-purpose flour

½ teaspoon salt

⅛ teaspoon freshly ground black pepper

½ teaspoon dried Italian herbs

8 ounces boneless, skinless turkey or chicken breast, cut into 1-inch strips

1 tablespoon vegetable oil

⅓ cup sun-dried tomatoes in oil, drained and chopped

1 clove garlic, minced

1 (10 ½-oz.) can condensed chicken broth

Remove and discard the mushroom stems. Soak the tops in hot water about 10 minutes. Drain, chop, and set aside. Cook the pasta according to package directions.

Meanwhile, combine the flour, salt, pepper, and herbs in a shallow bowl. Coat the turkey strips with the flour mixture. Heat the oil in a 10- to 12-inch skillet over medium heat; add the turkey. Cook, stirring, until lightly brown. Stir in the tomatoes, garlic, mushrooms, and undiluted broth. Cover and simmer 10 to 15 minutes. Serve turkey mixture over pasta.

Speedy Sausage Dinner

MAKES 4 OR 5 SERVINGS

A colorful yet tasty combination to serve when the family is clamoring for dinner and you are running late. Heat a loaf of French bread and toss a green salad while this simmers; get some help with setting the table and you can have dinner in 30 minutes.

6 to 8 ounces smoky cooked sausage links

1 (11-oz.) can Mexi-corn, undrained, or 1 (8 ¼-oz.) jar baby corn, drained

2 zucchini, thinly sliced

2 medium tomatoes, diced

1 clove garlic, crushed

½ teaspoon chili powder

¼ teaspoon salt

⅛ teaspoon freshly ground black pepper

Cut the sausage into ½-inch slices. Heat in a 10-inch skillet over medium heat. Stir in the corn, zucchini, tomatoes, garlic, chili powder, salt, and pepper. Simmer 10 to 15 minutes, stirring occasionally, to allow the flavors to combine.

Macaroni with Sun-Dried Tomatoes & Goat Cheese

MAKES 4 OR 5 SERVINGS

Thickened chicken broth forms an appetizing glaze over cooked pasta; finish with a sprinkling of pine nuts.

- 8 ounces uncooked medium elbow macaroni (about 2½ cups)
- 2 tablespoons butter or margarine
- 1 small onion, chopped
- 1 clove garlic, crushed
- 1 tablespoon cornstarch
- 1 cup chicken broth or bouillon
- ¼ cup sun-dried tomatoes in oil, drained and chopped
- 2 tablespoons chopped fresh parsley
- 2 tablespoons chopped fresh basil
- 2 ounces goat cheese, coarsely crumbled (about ¼ cup)
- ¼ cup pine nuts, toasted (see Tip, below)

Cook the pasta according to package directions; drain.

While the pasta cooks, melt the butter in a 10-inch skillet. Add the onion and garlic; sauté until softened, about 5 minutes. Dissolve the cornstarch in broth in a small bowl. Add to the skillet; stir in the tomatoes, parsley, and basil. Cook, stirring, until thickened. Remove from heat.

Toss the tomato mixture with cooked pasta. Sprinkle the top with the goat cheese, then the pine nuts.

TIP

To toast nuts: Preheat oven to 350F (175C). Spread nuts in a 9-inch cake or pie pan. Toast 5 to 8 minutes, or until golden. Or toast nuts in a dry skillet over low heat 3 to 4 minutes, stirring occasionally.

Turkey Tomato Sauté with Pasta

MAKES 4 TO 6 SERVINGS

Start with ground turkey to create a tempting and low-fat meal-in-a-skillet that's perfect for a family supper. Serve with steamed broccoli, if desired.

6 ounces uncooked pasta corkscrews or twists

1 tablespoon vegetable oil

1 pound ground turkey

1 small onion, chopped

½ teaspoon salt

⅛ teaspoon freshly ground black pepper

1 tablespoon minced fresh parsley

2 teaspoons grated fresh ginger

1 green or yellow bell pepper, sliced

12 to 14 cherry tomatoes, halved

1 cup sliced mushrooms

⅓ cup chicken broth

½ cup plain yogurt or sour cream

Cook the pasta according to package directions; drain.

Meanwhile, heat the oil in a 10-inch skillet. Add the turkey, onion, salt, pepper, parsley, and ginger. Cook over medium heat until turkey is done, stirring to break up turkey. Add the pasta to the turkey mixture with the bell pepper, tomatoes, mushrooms, broth, and yogurt. Heat until hot and serve.

VARIATION
Substitute bulk turkey sausage for the ground turkey. Omit the ginger. Prepare as directed.

Crockery Suppers

Electric slow cookers replicate the simmering stew pot. Sitting all

day on the back burner of the stove, it allows the food to slowly

cook, melding the flavors. Crockery cookers surround the food with

a low heat, making tougher meats tender without drying them out.

Try preparing Pot Luck Beans the next time you need to take a

dish to a picnic or tailgate party. Leave the beans in the pot and

place it in an ice chest or box packed in layers of newspaper.

It will stay hot for hours.

Beef & Mushroom Stew

Argentine Stuffed Steak Spirals

Cornish Hens with Fruited Wild Rice Stuffing

Crockery Posole

Beef Goulash

International Pork Strips

Herbed Potato & Garlic Soup

Herbed Rice & Pine Nut Chicken Roulades

Mediterranean Lamb Stew

Pot Luck Beans

Teriyaki Meatloaf

Mandarin Turkey & Vegetables

Beef & Mushroom Stew

MAKES 5 OR 6 SERVINGS

Round steak also results in an appetizing dish.

1 pound lean boneless beef stew meat, cut into ½-inch cubes

1 large onion, diced

2 cloves garlic, minced

1 (6-oz.) package sliced fresh mushrooms

1 stalk celery, diced

1 (8-oz.) can tomato sauce

½ teaspoon seasoned salt

1 tablespoon Worcestershire sauce

½ cup plain yogurt

2 tablespoons all-purpose flour

8 ounces uncooked noodles

2 tablespoons butter or margarine

2 tablespoons poppy seeds

Combine the meat, onion, garlic, mushrooms, celery, tomato sauce, salt, and Worcestershire sauce in a slow cooker; mix well.

Cover and cook on low 6 to 8 hours or until meat is tender. Turn slow cooker to high.

Combine the yogurt and flour in a small bowl; stir into meat mixture. Cover and cook on high 20 to 30 minutes, or until mixture is slightly thickened.

Cook noodles according to package directions; drain. Stir in butter and poppy seeds. Spoon meat mixture over noodles.

Argentine Stuffed Steak Spirals

MAKES 5 TO 6 SERVINGS

A variation on a well-known Latin American dish.

1½ pounds beef round steak, trimmed

¼ cup red wine vinegar

1 large clove garlic, minced

1 tablespoon minced fresh parsley

½ teaspoon freshly ground black pepper

¼ teaspoon ground dried thyme leaves

1 cup fresh French or Italian bread crumbs

¼ cup milk

1 (10-oz.) package frozen chopped spinach, thawed and drained

½ cup finely chopped green onions

6 ounces bulk Italian turkey sausage

¼ cup chopped fresh parsley

1 egg, slightly beaten

2 hard-cooked eggs, chopped

1 (0.87-oz.) package dry brown gravy mix

Parsley sprigs

Cut the steak into 3 or 4 pieces. Pound the steak between sheets of plastic wrap to ¼-inch thickness. In a shallow glass dish, combine the vinegar, garlic, minced parsley, pepper, and thyme. Add the steak; turn to coat. Set aside.

Soak the bread crumbs in milk. Add the spinach, onions, sausage, chopped parsley, and beaten egg; mix well.

Lay the steak pieces flat. Spread the spinach mixture evenly over steak pieces to within 1 inch of edges. Spread the chopped eggs on top of the spinach mixture, pressing in lightly. Starting at a long side roll up the steak pieces, jelly-roll fashion. Tie with string at about 1-inch intervals. Coat each roll with dry brown gravy mix.

Place the rolls, seam side down, in a slow cooker. Cover and cook on low 5 to 6 hours, or until meat is tender. Remove from cooker. Remove and discard string. Slice meat into 1-inch-thick slices. Place on a serving platter, overlapping the spirals slightly. Garnish with parsley sprigs.

Cornish Hens with Fruited Wild Rice Stuffing

MAKES 4 SERVINGS

Cornish game hens and fruit make an elegant entree for a special dinner or holiday meal.

> **2 Cornish game hens (about 1½ pounds each), thawed if frozen**
>
> **⅔ cup cooked wild rice**
>
> **1 medium apple, cored and coarsely chopped**
>
> **½ cup diced dried apricots**
>
> **¼ cup golden raisins**
>
> **2 tablespoons slivered almonds, toasted (see Tip, page 25)**
>
> **1 teaspoon ground ginger**
>
> **¼ teaspoon salt**
>
> **¼ teaspoon ground white pepper**
>
> **½ teaspoon freshly grated orange zest**
>
> **2 tablespoons apricot preserves**
>
> **¼ teaspoon sweet paprika**
>
> **1 teaspoon cornstarch**
>
> **2 tablespoons water**

Rinse the hens, drain and pat dry with paper towels. Trim any excess fat.

Combine the rice, apple, apricots, raisins, almonds, ginger, salt, pepper, and orange zest in a bowl. Spoon half of stuffing into each hen. Tie legs and wings close to body.

Melt the preserves in a small saucepan over low heat. Stir in the paprika; brush the hens with mixture. Put a rack in the bottom of a slow cooker. Place the hens on end, neck down, on the rack.

Cover and cook on low 6 to 7 hours, or until hens are tender. Remove hens from cooker; keep warm. Remove rack from cooker.

Turn control to high. In a small bowl, mix the cornstarch with the water; stir into cooking juices. Cover and cook on high 15 minutes or until slightly thickened. With shears or a sharp knife, cut the hens in half. Pass sauce for individual service.

Crockery Posole

MAKES 6 TO 8 SERVINGS

Using one can of yellow hominy and one can of white will give a more colorful posole.

> 1 pound boneless pork cubes
>
> 2 boneless skinless chicken breast halves, cut into 1-inch cubes
>
> 1 large onion, finely chopped
>
> 2 stalks celery, finely chopped
>
> 1 poblano chile, seeded and chopped (see Note, page 71)
>
> 1 (14½-oz.) can chicken broth
>
> 2 (15-oz.) cans hominy, drained
>
> 1 teaspoon dried oregano
>
> Sliced radishes, sliced green onions, salsa, or chopped jicama, to garnish

In a slow cooker, combine the pork, chicken, onion, celery, chile, broth, hominy, and oregano. Cover and cook on low for about 7 to 8 hours, or until meat is tender.

Serve in individual bowls. Garnish with radishes, green onion, salsa, or jicama.

Beef Goulash

MAKES 6 TO 8 SERVINGS

Slow cooking allows all the flavors to meld into a rich stew.

2 pounds boneless beef chuck steak, cut into 1½-inch cubes

1 large onion, sliced

2 cloves garlic, minced

1 to 2 tablespoons sweet paprika

½ teaspoon seasoned salt

1 teaspoon dried marjoram leaves

1 teaspoon sugar

½ teaspoon dry mustard

1 (14½-oz.) can beef broth

4 medium potatoes, peeled and cut into ½-inch cubes

1 large tomato, peeled, seeded, and finely chopped

2 teaspoons fresh lemon juice

2 tablespoons chopped fresh parsley

¼ cup all-purpose flour

¼ cup cold water

In a slow cooker, combine the beef, onion, garlic, paprika, salt, marjoram, sugar, mustard, broth, and potatoes. Top with tomato.

Cover and cook on low 8 to 10 hours, or until beef and potatoes are tender.

Turn control to high. Stir in the lemon juice and parsley. Combine the flour and water. Stir into cooker. Cover and cook on high 15 to 20 minutes, or until thickened.

International Pork Strips

Tender pork with a crispy topping of sliced pea pods.

- 4 to 5 lean boneless country-style pork ribs (about 1¼ pounds total)
- 1½ teaspoons crumbled dried oregano leaves
- 1 clove garlic, minced
- ½ teaspoon salt
- ¼ teaspoon freshly ground black pepper
- 1 cup mini tomatoes (see Note, below)
- 1 (10½-oz.) can condensed chicken broth
- ½ cup snow peas, cut into strips

Place the pork in a slow cooker. Top with the oregano, garlic, salt, pepper, and tomatoes. Pour the undiluted broth over all in pot.

Cover and cook on low 6 to 7 hours, or until pork is tender. Serve pork with cooking juices. Top with snow peas.

NOTE

Many new types of mini tomatoes are now available in the supermarkets and farmers markets. They range from tiny currant tomatoes to grape tomatoes to several sizes of pear and cherry tomatoes. Colors, shapes, and flavors vary. They're a fun way to add interest to cooked dishes and salads, or eat them as a snack.

Herbed Potato & Garlic Soup

MAKES 4 SERVINGS

Rich and full bodied, this soup is warming on a cold day.

1 whole head garlic (about 12 cloves)

1 small leek, trimmed and chopped

2 potatoes, peeled and diced

4 cups chicken broth

¼ teaspoon salt

¼ teaspoon ground dried thyme

¼ teaspoon ground white pepper

1 large bay leaf

1 whole dried red chile pepper

1 cup milk or half-and-half

¼ cup chopped fresh parsley

Separate the garlic into individual cloves; drop into boiling water and let cook 3 to 4 seconds. Drain. Cover with cold water; drain, and slip off skins; thinly slice.

In a slow cooker, combine the garlic, leek, potatoes, broth, salt, thyme, pepper, bay leaf, and chile. Cover and cook on low 7 to 8 hours, or until potatoes are tender.

Remove and discard the bay leaf and chile. With a potato masher, crush the potatoes.

Stir in the milk. Cover and cook on high 15 to 20 minutes, or until hot. Just before serving, stir in the parsley. Ladle soup into bowls.

Herbed Rice & Pine Nut Chicken Roulades

MAKES 4 SERVINGS

Chicken breasts are filled with pine nuts, mushrooms, herbs, and Parmesan cheese to make an entree special enough for company.

> 4 boneless, skinless chicken breast halves
>
> 1 cup cooked rice
>
> 4 tablespoons fresh lemon juice
>
> ¼ cup pine nuts, toasted (see Tip, page 25)
>
> 4 large fresh mushrooms, finely chopped
>
> ¼ cup chopped green onions
>
> ¼ cup fresh parsley, minced
>
> 3 tablespoons freshly shredded Parmesan cheese
>
> 1 tablespoon olive oil
>
> 1 teaspoon crushed dried oregano leaves
>
> ½ teaspoon salt
>
> ¼ teaspoon freshly ground black pepper
>
> ¼ teaspoon sweet paprika
>
> ½ cup chicken broth
>
> 1 tablespoon cornstarch
>
> 2 tablespoons water

Pound the chicken breasts between plastic wrap to ¼-inch thickness; set aside.

In a small bowl, combine the rice, 2 tablespoons of the lemon juice, pine nuts, mushrooms, onions, parsley, cheese, oil, oregano, and ¼ teaspoon of the salt; mix well. Place ⅓ cup of the mixture in the center of each chicken breast. Roll up and place in a slow cooker, seam side down. Sprinkle chicken evenly with the remaining ¼ teaspoon salt, the pepper, and paprika.

Mix together the broth and remaining 2 tablespoons lemon juice; pour around chicken.

Cover and cook on low 4 to 6 hours, or until chicken is tender. Remove the chicken from cooker; keep warm. Mix the cornstarch with water and stir into pan juices. Cover and cook on high 10 to 15 minutes, or until thickened. Spoon sauce on individual dinner plates and top with a chicken roll.

Mediterranean Lamb Stew

MAKES 6 SERVINGS

The green beans add color and fresh flavor to the stew.

1 ½ pounds boneless lamb stew meat

2 onions, chopped

1 ½ teaspoons ground cumin

½ teaspoon ground allspice

½ cup chopped fresh parsley

1 teaspoon salt

½ teaspoon freshly ground pepper

1 cup lentils

4 tomatoes, peeled, seeded, and chopped

½ cup beef broth

2 tablespoons white wine

1 (1-pound) bag frozen Italian green beans

In a slow cooker, thoroughly combine the lamb, onions, cumin, allspice, parsley, salt, pepper, and lentils. Top with tomatoes. Pour the broth and wine over all. Cover and cook on low 7 to 8 hours, or until lamb is tender.

Cook the beans according to package directions. Drain and stir beans into stew.

Pot Luck Beans

MAKES 6 TO 8 SERVINGS

These are a welcome addition to any picnic or party. They can make a meal by themselves with a tossed green salad or they can be served with barbecued beef or chicken.

1 pound smoked turkey sausage links, cut into ½-inch pieces

1 onion, chopped

1 tablespoon Worcestershire sauce

2 teaspoons dry mustard

2 teaspoons vinegar

½ teaspoon salt

⅓ cup packed light brown sugar

1 (8-oz.) can tomato sauce

1 (15-oz.) can kidney beans, drained

1 (30-oz.) can chili beans, undrained

1 (15-oz.) can butter beans, drained

Thoroughly combine all the ingredients in a slow cooker. Cover and cook on low about 6 hours. Serve hot.

Teriyaki Meatloaf

MAKES 5 OR 6 SERVINGS

Water chestnuts provide a surprising crunch in this meatloaf.

- 1 pound lean ground beef
- ⅓ cup quick-cooking rolled oats
- 1 egg, beaten slightly
- 1 small onion, grated
- 2 tablespoons soy sauce
- ½ teaspoon grated fresh ginger
- ¼ cup chopped canned water chestnuts
- ¼ cup prepared teriyaki sauce
- 1 cup cooked long-grain brown rice
- 1 tablespoon toasted sesame seeds

In a large bowl, combine all the ingredients, except the sesame seeds. Form into a 6-inch-round loaf. Press the sesame seeds into top. Place the loaf in a slow cooker.

Cover and cook on low about 4 hours. Remove from cooker and cut into slices.

Mandarin Turkey & Vegetables

MAKES 4 SERVINGS

Colorful vegetables accent this Chinese-inspired dish.

¾ pound boneless turkey breast, cut into 2 × ½-inch strips

2 carrots, peeled and coarsely shredded

1 onion, chopped

1 red bell pepper, cut into ½-inch squares

2 cups small broccoli flowerets

2 tablespoons soy sauce

1 clove garlic, minced

2 teaspoons grated fresh ginger

1 tablespoon light brown sugar

¼ teaspoon freshly ground black pepper

1 cup uncooked long-grain white rice

In a slow cooker, combine the turkey, carrots, onion, bell pepper, and broccoli. In a small bowl, combine the soy sauce, garlic, ginger, brown sugar, and black pepper. Pour over the turkey and vegetables. Cover and cook on low 6 to 7 hours, or until the turkey and vegetables are tender.

Cook the rice according to package directions. Place on a large platter. Spoon the turkey mixture over rice and serve.

Family Favorites

These recipes represent the everyday favorites that families share across the dinner table each night. They are universally beloved by even the pickiest eater. Who could turn down the elegant yet homey Crab Chalupas with Cilantro-Lime Dressing? Entice the fussiest diner with Ranch-Style Family Pie, a layered treat enlivened with creamy ranch salad dressing. Gather everyone round the table and enjoy.

Baked Fish with Herbed Stuffing

Crab Chalupas with Cilantro-Lime Dressing

Barbecued Chicken & Vegetable Skewers

Layered Corned Beef & Sauerkraut

Peanut Turkey Noodles

Pork, Potato, & Leek Bake

Roasted Garlic & Potato-Topped Meatloaf

Ranch-Style Family Pie

Skillet Chicken-Topped Spaghetti

Chicken Tortilla Casserole

Speedy Family Skillet

Turkey Tostadas

Turkey Burger Cheese Pie

Chicken & Rice Skillet

South-of-the-Border Lasagne

Baked Fish with Herbed Stuffing

MAKES 4 TO 6 SERVINGS

Any mild white fish fillet will work well with this dish.

1 (14½-oz.) can chicken broth

4 cups dry herb-seasoned stuffing

1 small onion, grated

¼ cup butter or margarine, melted

1 pound (½-inch-thick) fish fillets, cut into 4 to 6 pieces

1 (10½-oz.) can condensed cream of mushroom soup

8 fresh mushrooms, thinly sliced

¼ cup milk

Preheat oven to 400F (205C). Grease a 13 × 9-inch baking dish. In a large bowl, combine the broth, stuffing, onion, and butter. Let stand until most of the liquid is absorbed.

Place the fish in the center of prepared dish. Stir together the undiluted soup, mushrooms, and milk. Pour over fish. Arrange stuffing around edges of dish.

Cover and bake 20 minutes. Uncover and bake 10 to 15 minutes, or until fish flakes easily with a fork.

Crab Chalupas with Cilantro-Lime Dressing

Traditionally the masa was formed into boat-shaped chalupas; here we shape the masa in easier-to-cook circles.

¼ cup butter or margarine, softened

1½ cups masa harina (see Note, below)

¼ teaspoon salt

⅛ teaspoon freshly ground black pepper

⅔ cup water

1 (15- to 16-oz.) can refried black beans

2 tablespoons vegetable oil

1 cup (4 ounces) shredded Monterey Jack cheese

¾ pound cooked crabmeat

6 cups mixed baby salad greens

1 large avocado, sliced

¼ cup sour cream

2 tablespoons chopped fresh chives

CILANTRO-LIME DRESSING

½ cup loosely packed cilantro leaves

¼ cup vegetable oil

2 tablespoons fresh lime juice

½ teaspoon sugar

¼ teaspoon salt

⅛ teaspoon freshly ground black pepper

Beat together the butter, masa harina, salt, and pepper in a medium bowl. Stir in the water to make a stiff dough.

Divide into 4 parts and pat each into a ¼-inch-thick, round chalupa. Set aside.

Prepare the dressing: In a blender or food processor, process all the ingredients until pureed; set aside.

Heat the beans in a small saucepan; keep warm. Heat the oil in a large skillet over medium heat. Add the chalupas and cook on both sides until lightly browned. Place each on a serving plate. Spread each chalupa with one fourth of the beans and sprinkle with one fourth of the cheese. Divide the crab among the chalupas.

In a large bowl, toss the dressing with the salad greens. Divide among the chalupas. Arrange the avocado slices on the greens. Spoon the sour cream on each. Sprinkle with chives.

NOTE

Masa harina is the flour made from dried masa, which is dried corn that has been cooked in lime water and ground. It is used for making corn tortillas and tamales. Masa harina is available near the flour and cornmeal in most supermarkets.

Barbecued Chicken & Vegetable Skewers

MAKES 4 SERVINGS

If baby pattypan squash aren't available you can substitute six regular size ones and cut them into quarters.

> 4 boneless, skinless chicken breast halves, cut into 1- to 1½-inch pieces
>
> ½ cup bottled barbecue sauce
>
> 12 baby pattypan squash, cut in half
>
> 24 red cherry tomatoes
>
> 1 red onion, cut into wedges
>
> 1 (27-oz.) can baked beans

Preheat broiler or grill. Combine the chicken and barbecue sauce in a medium bowl. Steam the squash 2 to 3 minutes. Thread the chicken, squash, tomatoes, and onion on 8 (10- to 12-inch) skewers. Brush with any remaining sauce.

Place skewers in a broiler pan or on a grill 4 to 5 inches from heat. Cook 4 to 5 minutes. Turn and cook 3 to 4 minutes or until chicken is cooked through.

Meanwhile, in a medium saucepan, heat the beans. Transfer the beans to a large platter. Arrange the skewers over the beans.

Layered Corned Beef & Sauerkraut

MAKES 4 TO 6 SERVINGS

This is a super idea for using the remainder of a corned beef roast.

- ¾ to 1 pound cooked corned beef, sliced
- 5 medium carrots, peeled and thinly sliced
- 1 medium onion, sliced
- 5 medium potatoes, peeled and sliced
- ½ teaspoon caraway seeds
- 1 (15- to 16-oz.) can sauerkraut, drained
- 1 tablespoon sweet-hot mustard
- 1 (10½-oz.) can condensed chicken broth

Preheat oven to 375F (190C). Grease a 13 × 9-inch baking dish. Arrange the corned beef in prepared dish. Top with carrots, then onion, potatoes, and caraway seeds. Spread sauerkraut over the top. Stir the mustard into the broth. Pour over the sauerkraut.

Cover and bake 1 to 1¼ hours, or until the potatoes and carrots are tender.

Peanut Turkey Noodles

MAKES 4 OR 5 SERVINGS

Glamorize yesterday's turkey by creating this exciting noodle dish.

8 ounces egg noodles

1 tablespoon vegetable oil

¼ cup coarsely chopped peanuts

2 green onions, sliced

2 tablespoons chopped crystallized ginger

⅓ cup smooth peanut butter

¼ cup soy sauce

¼ teaspoon crushed red pepper flakes

1 clove garlic, minced

1 tablespoon honey

4 teaspoons cornstarch

1 cup chicken broth

2 cups cooked bite-size turkey pieces

2 oranges, peeled and cut into chunks

1 cup snow peas, cut in half

Cook the noodles according to package directions; drain.

Meanwhile, heat the oil in a large skillet over medium heat. Add the peanuts and onions. Stir-fry 2 or 3 minutes. Stir in the ginger, peanut butter, soy sauce, pepper flakes, garlic, and honey. Cook, stirring, until well blended.

Dissolve the cornstarch in the broth. Add to the peanut mixture with the turkey; cook, stirring, until bubbly.

Transfer noodles to a serving dish. Spoon turkey mixture over noodles. Top with oranges and peas.

Pork, Potato, & Leek Bake

MAKES 5 OR 6 SERVINGS

Grandma's old-fashioned baked pork chops and potatoes are updated with today's ingredients.

¼ cup soy sauce

1 tablespoon Dijon mustard

¼ cup butter or margarine, melted

1 clove garlic, minced

2 leeks, sliced

5 or 6 medium Yukon gold potatoes, peeled and sliced

4 medium shiitake mushrooms, sliced

5 or 6 pork chops (1½ to 2 pounds)

⅛ teaspoon freshly ground black pepper

Preheat oven to 375F (190C). Grease a 13 × 9-inch baking dish. In a small bowl, combine the soy sauce, mustard, butter, and garlic; set aside.

Arrange alternate layers of leeks and potatoes in the bottom of the prepared dish. Top with the mushrooms, then the pork chops. Season with the pepper. Spoon the soy mixture over all.

Cover and bake about 30 minutes. Uncover and bake 30 minutes, or until the potatoes are tender.

Roasted Garlic & Potato-Topped Meatloaf

MAKES 5 OR 6 SERVINGS

An entire head of garlic makes this dish redolent of garlic. Use just a few cloves if you prefer a milder garlic flavor.

1½ pounds lean ground beef

1 cup fresh soft bread crumbs

1 egg, slightly beaten

¾ cup milk

1 tablespoon Worcestershire sauce

1 small onion, minced

1 teaspoon salt

¼ teaspoon freshly ground black pepper

1 head of garlic

½ teaspoon olive or vegetable oil

6 medium red-skinned potatoes, each cut into 8 wedges

Boiling water, to cover

¼ cup butter or margarine

Preheat oven to 350F (175C). Grease a 13 × 9-inch baking pan. Combine the beef, bread crumbs, egg, ½ cup of the milk, the Worcestershire sauce, onion, ½ teaspoon of the salt, and the pepper. Form into a loaf and place in prepared pan. Cut about ¼ inch off the top of the garlic tips. Place in pan with meatloaf. Drizzle the oil over the cut garlic.

Bake 1 hour. Remove garlic and meatloaf. Preheat broiler.

Meanwhile, in a large saucepan, cook the potatoes in boiling water until tender, 20 to 25 minutes; drain.

Squeeze the pulp from the garlic and chop. Add to the potatoes; mash potatoes and garlic. Stir in the remaining ¼ cup milk, the butter, and the remaining ½ teaspoon salt. Spread over hot meatloaf.

Broil 6 to 8 inches from heat until lightly browned on top. Cut into slices and serve.

Ranch-Style Family Pie

MAKES ABOUT 6 SERVINGS

This will soon be a favorite in your recipe repertoire.

1 pound lean ground beef

2 tomatoes, thinly sliced

1 (10-oz.) package frozen chopped broccoli, cooked and drained

½ teaspoon seasoned salt

¼ teaspoon freshly ground black pepper

1 cup (4 ounces) shredded Monterey Jack cheese

1 cup sour cream

½ cup prepared creamy ranch salad dressing

1 cup milk

1 egg

2 cups buttermilk baking mix

2 green onions, chopped

Preheat oven to 375F (190C). Grease a 13 × 9-inch baking dish. Cook the beef in a large nonstick skillet over medium-high heat until no longer pink, stirring to break up. Spoon into prepared dish. Top with the tomatoes and broccoli. Sprinkle with the salt and pepper.

Combine the cheese, sour cream, and dressing in a small bowl. Spread over broccoli. Whisk together the milk, egg, baking mix, and onions. Pour over contents of baking dish.

Bake 25 to 30 minutes, or until top is lightly browned.

Skillet Chicken—Topped Spaghetti

MAKES 4 TO 6 SERVINGS

Tired of spaghetti and meatballs? Try this for a quick change.

8 ounces uncooked spaghetti or fusilli

¼ cup all-purpose flour

¼ teaspoon salt

¼ teaspoon freshly ground pepper

4 to 6 boneless chicken thighs

1 tablespoon vegetable oil

4 to 6 fresh mushrooms, sliced

1 (28-oz.) jar tomato pasta sauce with herbs

⅓ cup freshly grated Parmesan cheese

Cook the pasta according to package directions; drain.

Meanwhile, combine the flour, salt, and pepper in a plastic bag. Add the chicken and shake to coat.

Heat the oil in 12-inch skillet or electric skillet on medium-high heat. Add the chicken and fry until lightly browned, 2 to 3 minutes on each side. Stir in the mushrooms. Cook, stirring, over low heat 1 to 2 minutes.

Stir in the pasta sauce and cook until hot and bubbly and chicken is tender, stirring occasionally. Transfer the pasta to a large platter. Pour chicken and sauce over pasta. Top with Parmesan cheese.

Chicken Tortilla Casserole

MAKES 4 TO 6 SERVINGS

An old favorite has been updated with flavor-adding vegetables.

1 tablespoon vegetable oil

1 large onion, chopped

2 large poblano or other mild fresh chiles, seeded and chopped

2 cloves garlic, minced

3 tomatillos, husked and chopped (see Note, below)

1 large potato, peeled and cut into ½-inch cubes

2 tablespoons all-purpose flour

1 (14½-oz.) can chicken broth

Kernels from 1 ear of corn (about ½ cup)

⅓ cup finely chopped fresh cilantro

2 cups cubed cooked chicken

⅓ cup sour cream

6 (6-inch) corn tortillas, cut into quarters

1½ cups (6 ounces) shredded Monterey Jack cheese

Preheat oven to 375F (190C). Grease a 2½-quart casserole dish. Heat the oil in a large saucepan over medium heat. Add the onion, chiles, and garlic and cook until onion is softened, 5 to 10 minutes. Add the tomatillos, potato, and flour; stir to combine. Stir in the broth. Cook over medium-low heat, stirring occasionally, about 15 minutes, or until potato is tender. Add the corn, cilantro, and chicken. Stir in the sour cream.

Spoon ½ cup of the chicken mixture in the bottom of prepared casserole. Arrange 8 tortilla quarters over mixture. Spread one third of the remaining chicken mixture on the tortillas. Sprinkle with one third of the cheese. Repeat layers with remaining ingredients, ending with cheese.

Bake 25 to 30 minutes, or until hot and bubbly.

NOTE

When you remove the papery husks from the tomatillos, they are slightly sticky. To remove the sticky coating, rinse the tomatillos in very warm water. Fresh tomatillos should be firm and green with tight-fitting husks. Tomatillos are available both fresh and canned.

Speedy Family Skillet

MAKES 4 OR 5 SERVINGS

These sausages are bite-size miniatures of the regular smoked sausage links. Look for them in the deli or meat section of the supermarket.

- 1 (16-oz.) package small cocktail-size smoked sausages
- 1 onion, sliced
- 2 zucchini, chopped
- 3 yellow pattypan squash, cut into thin wedges
- 3 plum tomatoes, chopped
- 1 clove garlic, minced
- 1 teaspoon chili powder
- ¼ teaspoon salt
- ¼ teaspoon freshly ground black pepper
- 1 (16-oz.) can baked beans, undrained
- 1 (15-oz.) can whole-kernel corn, drained

Combine the sausage, onion, zucchini, pattypan squash, tomatoes, garlic, chili powder, salt, and pepper in a large skillet over medium heat. Simmer, stirring occasionally, until vegetables are tender, 10 to 15 minutes.

Stir in the beans and corn and heat until hot.

Turkey Tostadas

MAKES 4 SERVINGS

A dab of sour cream on top of each serving results in an interesting flavor surprise.

- 1 medium onion, chopped
- 1 clove garlic, minced
- 1 tablespoon butter or margarine
- 1 small jalapeño chile, seeded and minced
- 4 plum tomatoes, chopped
- ½ teaspoon salt
- 1 tablespoon chopped fresh cilantro
- 2 cups cooked turkey strips (about 10 ounces)
- ⅓ cup vegetable oil
- 4 (8-inch) flour tortillas
- 1 (16-oz.) can refried beans, heated
- 1 cup (4 ounces) shredded Colby-Jack cheese
- ¼ cup sour cream

Combine the onion, garlic, and butter in a medium saucepan over medium heat. Cook, stirring occasionally, 3 or 4 minutes. Add the chile, tomatoes, salt, and cilantro. Simmer about 5 minutes. Stir in the turkey; heat several minutes or until hot.

Meanwhile, heat the oil in a large skillet. Add the tortillas, one at a time. Cook until lightly browned and crisp on one side; turn and brown other side. Drain on paper towels. Place the tortillas on individual serving plates. Spread each with one fourth of the refried beans. Top each with one fourth of the turkey mixture, then one fourth of the cheese. Add a dollop of sour cream.

Turkey Burger Cheese Pie

MAKES 8 SERVINGS

One of my favorite individual casseroles, it has an easy golden biscuit topping.

12 ounces ground turkey

½ teaspoon salt

⅛ teaspoon freshly ground pepper

½ teaspoon chili powder

2 medium tomatoes, sliced

1 cup (4 ounces) shredded Cheddar cheese

1 cup light sour cream

½ cup light mayonnaise

1 tablespoon chopped green onion

⅔ cup milk

1 egg, slightly beaten

1 ½ cups buttermilk baking mix

Cook the turkey in a 10-inch nonstick skillet over medium heat until lightly browned, stirring to break up. Add the salt, pepper, and chili powder; set aside.

Preheat oven to 375F (190C). Spoon the turkey into bottom of 8 (4 ½-inch) greased individual tart pans. Top with the tomato slices. Combine the cheese, sour cream, mayonnaise, and onions in a small bowl. Spoon the cheese mixture over the tomatoes.

Process the milk, egg, and baking mix until smooth in a food processor or mix in a small bowl to form a soft dough. Spoon equal amounts of batter on top of each pie.

Bake 18 to 20 minutes, or until golden brown.

VARIATION

Add 1 teaspoon dried oregano leaves and ½ teaspoon coarsely ground black pepper to the baking mix before adding the milk and egg.

Chicken & Rice Skillet

MAKES 6 SERVINGS

A skillet dish that incorporates so many popular flavors that it will become one of your favorites.

3 bacon slices, chopped

6 chicken thighs or chicken breast halves

1 cup uncooked long-grain rice

1 onion, cut into 6 wedges

1 yellow or green bell pepper, sliced

3 medium tomatoes, chopped

½ teaspoon salt

⅛ teaspoon freshly ground black pepper

1 cup chicken broth

1 tablespoon chopped fresh parsley

Cook the bacon in a 12-inch skillet until almost crisp. Drain off some fat, if desired. Add the chicken; cook until lightly browned.

Stir in the rice, onion, bell pepper, tomatoes, salt, black pepper, and broth. Cover and simmer until the chicken and rice are tender, 30 to 40 minutes. Sprinkle parsley over top.

South-of-the-Border Lasagne

Accompany this hearty dish with a tossed green salad enhanced with chunks of avocado.

8 ounces uncooked lasagne noodles

1 pound lean ground beef

2 medium tomatoes, chopped

1 onion, chopped

1 green bell pepper, chopped

1 clove garlic, crushed

1 (10- to 12-oz.) jar enchilada sauce

8 ounces ricotta cheese

1 (16-oz.) can chili beans in zesty sauce, undrained

2 cups (8 ounces) shredded jalapeño Jack cheese

Chopped cilantro

Cook the lasagne noodles according to package directions; drain. Cover with cold water; drain just before combining with other ingredients.

Preheat oven to 350F (175C). Grease a 13 × 9-inch baking dish. Lightly brown the beef in a large skillet, stirring to break up. Add the tomatoes, onion, bell pepper, and garlic, cover, and simmer 10 minutes. Stir in the enchilada sauce.

Arrange one third of the drained noodles on the bottom of prepared dish. Spoon one third of the sauce over the noodles, then layer one third of the ricotta cheese, beans, and Jack cheese over the sauce. Repeat layers, ending with Jack cheese on top.

Bake 35 to 40 minutes, or until bubbly. Sprinkle with cilantro; cut into squares.

Meatless Marvels

There are many reasons for choosing a vegetarian meal. For some people it is a matter of personal beliefs. Other people are electing to avoid meats for health reasons. Other practical diners realize that meatless menus are easy on the budget. Beans and grains are good protein sources without the saturated animal fats. Whether you choose a soy-based recipe like Tofu Tortilla Soup or a peanut butter–pasta combo like Easy Soba Noodles, these meatless meals provide a wide range of vegetarian options.

Asparagus Cheese Pie

Baked Rajas de Poblanos

Baked Macaroni & Cheese

Easy Soba Noodles

Falafel Pockets

Italian Macaroni & Cheese

Pesto Lasagne

Tofu Tortilla Soup

Vegetable Cannelloni

Garden-Fresh Soybean Burgers

Herbed Pinto Bake

Three-Cheese Tomato Flan

Corn Custard Tomato Cups

Corn, Bean, & Tomato Bowl

Asparagus Cheese Pie

MAKES 4 TO 6 SERVINGS

A springtime luncheon treat, make this when asparagus is at its freshest and is at its lowest price.

½ cup butter, chilled

1⅔ cups all-purpose flour

⅛ teaspoon salt

2 tablespoons vegetable oil

⅓ cup cold water

5 to 6 ounces asparagus, trimmed and cut into 1-inch slices

1 cup small-curd cottage cheese

1 egg, beaten slightly

2 ounces blue cheese, broken into small pieces (½ cup)

2 green onions, sliced

Cut the butter into ½-inch pieces. Combine the flour and salt in a medium bowl; add the butter. With a pastry blender, cut in the butter until the mixture resembles oatmeal. Stir in the oil and cold water just until the dough will form a ball. Wrap in plastic wrap or foil; refrigerate at least 1 hour.

Preheat oven to 400F (205C). Roll out the dough on a lightly floured surface. Fit into a 9-inch pie plate; flute edges and prick bottom and sides.

Bake crust 10 to 15 minutes, or until lightly browned, remove from oven. Reduce oven to 350F (175C).

Meanwhile, cook the asparagus in boiling water until crisp-tender, 5 to 7 minutes; drain. Combine the asparagus, cottage cheese, egg, blue cheese, and onions in a medium bowl. Spoon cheese mixture into baked pastry shell.

Bake 35 to 40 minutes, or until filling is set. Cut into wedges and serve warm.

Baked Rajas de Poblanos

MAKES 4 SERVINGS

Roasting and peeling the chiles give this a smoky spicy infusion.

4 poblano chiles (see Note, below)

1 tablespoon vegetable oil

1 large onion, chopped

1 tablespoon all-purpose flour

1 (8-oz.) can tomato sauce

1 ½ cups half-and-half

8 (6-inch) corn tortillas, cut into strips

2 cups (8 ounces) shredded Monterey Jack cheese

Preheat broiler. Place the chiles on a baking sheet. Broil 4 to 5 inches from heat, turning until skin blisters and turns dark. Place in a paper bag; let sit 10 to 15 minutes. Cut the chiles in half lengthwise and remove seeds. Discard the skin and cut into ½-inch-wide strips; set aside.

Preheat oven to 350F (175C). Grease a 2-quart baking dish. Heat the oil in a medium saucepan over medium heat. Add the onion and cook until translucent. Sprinkle with the flour; stir to combine. Stir in the tomato sauce and half-and-half. Cook over medium heat until bubbly.

Pour ½ cup of the hot sauce into prepared dish. Add half of the tortillas, chiles, and cheese. Pour half of the remaining sauce over the cheese, then add remaining tortillas and chiles. Pour the remaining sauce over the chiles and top with the remaining cheese.

Bake 30 minutes, or until bubbly.

NOTE

Poblano chiles are full-flavored, dark green chiles that range from mild to hot in spiciness. They are excellent for stuffing because they are wide at the stem end and 4 to 5 inches long.

Baked Macaroni & Cheese

MAKES 4 SERVINGS

No ordinary macaroni and cheese, this is an old favorite with a new twist.

8 ounces uncooked rigatoni or ziti

2 tablespoons butter or margarine

2 tablespoons all-purpose flour

2 cups milk or half-and-half

1 tablespoon Dijon mustard

2 tablespoons chopped sun-dried tomatoes in oil, drained

2 eggs, beaten slightly

1 (11-oz.) can white and yellow corn, drained

1 (4-oz.) can diced green chiles, drained

1 cup (4 ounces) shredded Monterey Jack cheese

Cook the pasta according to package directions. Drain; set aside.

Preheat oven to 350F (175C). Grease a 1½- to 2-quart baking dish. Melt the butter in a medium saucepan over medium heat. Add the flour; cook, stirring, until bubbly. Stir in the milk, mustard, and tomatoes. Cook over medium heat, stirring occasionally, until thickened; remove from heat.

Combine the eggs, corn, chiles, and pasta in a large bowl. Slowly stir the sauce into the pasta. Mix thoroughly. Pour into prepared dish. Sprinkle with cheese.

Bake 40 to 45 minutes, or until bubbly and top is brown.

Easy Soba Noodles

MAKES 4 SERVINGS

Fresh Japanese soba noodles are found in the refrigerated section of most super-markets. Fresh fettuccini may be substituted.

½ cup creamy peanut butter

¼ cup soy sauce

2 tablespoons fresh lime juice

3 tablespoons honey

2 tablespoons seasoned rice vinegar

1 tablespoon Worcestershire sauce

1 tablespoon spicy brown mustard

1¼ to 1½ pounds uncooked fresh soba noodles

2 cups broccoli flowerets

2 carrots, peeled and cut into thin strips

2 cups sugar snap peas, trimmed

1 tablespoon black sesame seeds or toasted white sesame seeds

Whisk together the peanut butter, soy sauce, lime juice, honey, vinegar, Worcestershire sauce, and mustard in a medium bowl; set aside.

Bring 3 quarts of water to a boil in a 4-quart saucepan. Add the noodles, broccoli, and carrots. Cook for amount of time indicated on the noodle package. Add the peas during the last 1 minute of cooking; drain.

Toss the noodles and vegetables with the peanut butter sauce. Sprinkle with the sesame seeds. Serve warm or at room temperature.

Falafel Pockets

MAKES 4 SERVINGS

The cucumber adds a refreshing note to this Middle Eastern sandwich favorite.

1 Japanese cucumber (see Note, below)

1 (15-oz.) can garbanzo beans, drained

1 egg

1 tablespoon fresh lemon juice

1 clove garlic, minced

¼ cup coarsely chopped fresh parsley

¼ teaspoon salt

¼ teaspoon freshly ground black pepper

⅛ teaspoon cayenne pepper

2 tablespoons vegetable oil

½ cup plain yogurt

2 teaspoons chopped fresh mint leaves

1 teaspoon sesame oil

2 (7-inch) pita bread rounds, cut in half crosswise

4 romaine or butter lettuce leaves

Peel and coarsely shred the cucumber. Place in a strainer to let liquid drain until ready to serve.

In a blender or food processor, combine the beans, egg, lemon juice, garlic, parsley, salt, black pepper, and cayenne until smooth. Form into 4 oval patties, about 3 × 6 inches.

Heat the vegetable oil in a large skillet over medium-high heat. Add the falafel patties and fry until brown on both sides, 5 to 10 minutes.

Stir together the yogurt, mint, and sesame oil in a small bowl.

Place a patty in each pita half. Add some of the drained cucumber and some lettuce to each sandwich. Drizzle sandwiches with the yogurt sauce. Serve immediately.

NOTE
Japanese cucumbers are long dark green cucumbers similar to the English or European greenhouse varieties but shorter in length and smaller in diameter. If a Japanese cucumber isn't available use any small cucumber or use half of a large cucumber with its seeds removed.

Italian Macaroni & Cheese

MAKES 4 SERVINGS

To add extra eye appeal, use rainbow-colored corkscrew noodles.

8 ounces uncooked corkscrew pasta or elbow macaroni

1 tablespoon olive or vegetable oil

2 tablespoons butter or margarine

2 tablespoons all-purpose flour

1 cup milk

2 zucchini, shredded

1 teaspoon dry mustard

½ teaspoon salt

2 cups (8 ounces) shredded mozzarella cheese

1 large tomato, thinly sliced

3 tablespoons chopped fresh basil

2 tablespoons chopped fresh parsley

½ cup ricotta cheese

½ cup freshly grated Parmesan cheese

Cook the pasta according to package directions; drain and toss with the oil.

Meanwhile, melt the butter in a medium saucepan over medium-high heat. Add the flour and stir until bubbly. Stir in the milk, zucchini, mustard, and salt. Bring to a boil; reduce heat to low. Add the mozzarella cheese, stirring until melted.

Preheat oven to 350F (175C). Grease a 2-quart baking dish. Put half of the cooked pasta in prepared dish. Spoon half of the cheese sauce over the pasta. Top with half of the tomato. Combine the basil, parsley, and ricotta cheese. Dot over the tomato.

Repeat with remaining pasta, cheese sauce, tomato, and ricotta mixture. Sprinkle the top with the Parmesan cheese.

Bake 30 to 40 minutes, or until bubbly and top is brown.

Pesto Lasagne

MAKE ABOUT 6 SERVINGS

If you have a favorite pesto recipe and a garden with fresh basil, substitute your own sauce for the prepared sauce.

8 ounces uncooked lasagna noodles

1 (28-oz.) can Italian-style cut-up tomatoes

1 (8-oz.) can tomato sauce

1 (6-oz.) can tomato paste

1 teaspoon dried oregano

1 (15-oz.) carton ricotta cheese

1 (7-oz.) carton prepared pesto sauce (about ¾ cup)

1 (10-oz.) package frozen chopped broccoli or spinach, thawed and drained

2 eggs, slightly beaten

¼ teaspoon freshly ground black pepper

2 cups (8 ounces) shredded mozzarella cheese

⅓ cup freshly grated Parmesan cheese

Preheat oven to 350F (175C). Grease a 13 × 9-inch baking dish. Cook the lasagne noodles according to package directions; drain. Cover with cold water; drain just before combining with other ingredients.

Combine the tomatoes, tomato sauce, tomato paste, and oregano in a medium bowl. Combine the ricotta cheese, pesto, broccoli, eggs, and pepper in a medium bowl.

Spread ½ cup of the sauce on the bottom of the prepared dish. Arrange one third of the noodles on the sauce. Spread half of the ricotta mixture on the noodles. Sprinkle with ½ cup of the mozzarella cheese. Add another layer of noodles. Spoon half of the remaining sauce over the noodles. Cover with remaining ricotta mixture and ½ cup of the mozzarella cheese. Arrange remaining noodles on cheese. Pour the remaining sauce over the noodles. Top with the remaining 1 cup of mozzarella cheese and the Parmesan cheese.

Bake 35 to 40 minutes, or until bubbly. Let stand 10 minutes before serving.

Tofu Tortilla Soup

MAKES 4 SERVINGS

Taco sauce is usually smooth and thick. Because it comes in varying degrees of heat, choose the one that suits your taste for spiciness.

7 to 8 ounces firm tofu, cut into small cubes (about 1 ¼ cups)

⅓ cup bottled hot or mild taco sauce

2 (6-inch) corn tortillas

1 tablespoon vegetable oil

1 large onion, chopped

2 cloves garlic, minced

1 to 2 jalapeño chiles, halved, seeded, and cut into thin strips

3 carrots, peeled and chopped

2 stalks celery, chopped

2 (14-oz.) cans vegetable broth

Kernels cut and scraped from 2 ears of corn

⅓ cup chopped fresh cilantro

1 avocado, chopped

Stir together the tofu and taco sauce in a small bowl; set aside.

Preheat oven to 400F (205C). Cut the tortillas in half, then into ¼-inch-wide strips. Arrange the tortilla strips in a single layer on a baking sheet. Toast strips 5 to 8 minutes, stirring once.

Heat the oil in 4-quart saucepan over medium heat. Stir in the onion, garlic, chiles, carrots, and celery. Cook until vegetables are softened, about 10 minutes, stirring occasionally. Stir in the broth. Simmer, covered, 15 to 20 minutes, or until vegetables are tender.

Stir in reserved tofu with sauce, corn, and cilantro. Heat until hot. Ladle soup into bowls. Top with the tortilla strips and avocado.

Vegetable Cannelloni

MAKES 4 OR 5 SERVINGS

Make good use of fresh vegetables from your garden or the farmers market.

8 to 10 uncooked cannelloni or manicotti shells

1 tablespoon butter or margarine, melted

¼ cup water

3 cups chopped fresh broccoli or 1 (10-oz.) package frozen chopped broccoli

1 cup ricotta cheese

¼ cup freshly grated Parmesan cheese

1 egg yolk, slightly beaten

¼ teaspoon ground nutmeg

⅛ teaspoon ground ginger

1 tablespoon vegetable oil

2 medium carrots, peeled and shredded

2 green onions, finely chopped

1 medium zucchini, shredded

1 stalk celery with leaves, finely chopped

¼ teaspoon salt

⅛ teaspoon freshly ground black pepper

Cook the pasta shells according to package directions; drain. Toss with the butter.

Meanwhile, bring the water to a boil in a small saucepan; add the broccoli. Cover and simmer until almost tender, about 5 minutes; drain.

Preheat oven to 325F (165C). Grease an 11 × 7-inch baking pan. Combine the ricotta cheese, Parmesan cheese, egg yolk, nutmeg, ginger, and broccoli in a medium bowl. Spoon the ricotta mixture into the cooked shells. Place in prepared pan; set aside.

Heat the oil in a medium saucepan over medium heat. Stir in the carrots, onions, zucchini, celery, salt, and pepper. Cook until vegetables are tender, about 10 minutes, stirring occasionally. Spoon the vegetables over the filled cannelloni.

Bake 20 minutes, or until hot. Serve immediately.

Garden-Fresh
Soybean Burgers

MAKES 4 SERVINGS

If the mixture sticks to your hands while forming the patties, just slightly dampen your fingers with a little water.

½ cup uncooked brown rice blend or brown basmanti rice

4 dried shiitake mushrooms

1 cup shelled fresh or frozen green soybeans (edamame)

1 medium potato, peeled and cut into 1-inch chunks

¼ cup chopped pecans, toasted (see Tip, page 25)

¼ cup chopped fresh parsley

1 tablespoon grated onion

1 tablespoon chopped fresh basil

¼ teaspoon salt

¼ teaspoon freshly ground black pepper

2 tablespoons vegetable oil

4 whole-grain rolls or hamburger buns

4 leaves butter lettuce

Spicy brown mustard, to taste

Cook the rice according to package directions; set aside to cool. Soak the mushrooms in boiling water to cover 20 minutes; drain. Remove the stems and discard. Chop the caps; set aside. Cook the soybeans according to package directions. Drain; set aside.

Cook the potato in water in a medium saucepan over medium heat about 20 minutes, or until tender; drain. Mash with a fork or potato masher; set aside.

In a food processor, combine the mushrooms, rice, soybeans, pecans, parsley, onion, and basil. Process until finely chopped but not pureed. Stir in the potato, salt, and pepper. Form into 4 (4-inch-diameter) patties.

Heat the oil in large skillet or griddle over medium heat. Add the patties and cook about 5 minutes on each side or until brown. Place each patty on the bottom half of a roll. Add the lettuce and roll tops. Serve with the mustard.

Herbed Pinto Bake

MAKES ABOUT 6 SERVINGS

These dried pintos don't need to be soaked for hours, just simmer until tender and then bake.

1 pound dried pinto beans

1 tablespoon chopped fresh parsley

2 teaspoons chopped fresh oregano

1 teaspoon chopped fresh thyme

6 cups water

1 jalapeño chile, seeded and finely chopped

½ teaspoon salt

1 medium onion, chopped

1 clove garlic, minced

1 medium tomato, peeled and diced

1 (10½-oz.) can condensed chicken broth

¼ cup sour cream

¼ cup seasoned dry bread crumbs

Combine the beans, parsley, oregano, and thyme in a 4- to 6-quart pot. Add the water. Cover and simmer until beans are tender, 1 to 1¼ hours; drain.

Preheat oven to 325F (165C). Grease a 2½- to 3-quart baking dish. Add the beans, chile, salt, onion, garlic, tomato, and undiluted chicken broth to prepared dish.

Cover and bake 1 hour. Top with the sour cream, then the bread crumbs. Bake about 20 minutes, or until bread crumbs are brown.

Three-Cheese Tomato Flan

This easy flan uses cracker crumbs to make the crust. The flavor is at its best when the flan is warm or at room temperature.

1 cup crushed sesame crackers (20 to 24 crackers)

3 tablespoons butter or margarine, melted

8 ounces (1 cup) ricotta cheese

4 ounces blue cheese, crumbled (⅔ cup)

3 ounces light cream cheese, softened

2 eggs, slightly beaten

¼ cup sun-dried tomatoes in oil, drained and chopped

Sour cream (optional)

Chopped chives (optional)

Preheat oven to 350F (175C). Combine the cracker crumbs and margarine in a small bowl. Press the cracker mixture on the bottom of a 9-inch quiche pan. Bake 8 to 10 minutes, or until golden.

Combine the cheeses in a medium bowl. Beat in the eggs. Stir in the tomatoes. Carefully spoon over hot crust.

Bake 25 to 30 minutes, or until filling is set. Cool; cut into wedges. Garnish each slice with a dab of sour cream and chives, if desired.

VARIATION
Cut into 16 to 18 thin wedges. Serve as an appetizer.

Corn Custard Tomato Cups

MAKES 4 SERVINGS

This updated version of corn pudding is baked in a tomato shell. Do not over-cook these or the tomatoes will fall apart.

4 tomatoes (6 to 7 ounces each)

2 eggs

1 teaspoon sugar

¼ teaspoon salt

⅛ teaspoon freshly ground pepper

1 (8-oz.) can whole-kernel corn, well drained

1 teaspoon minced onion

⅓ cup milk or evaporated milk

¼ cup shredded Swiss cheese

Chopped fresh parsley

Cut off a slice, about ½-inch thick, across the top of each tomato. With a spoon, scoop out and discard all seeds and pulp, leaving the tomato shell. Turn upside down to drain on paper towels.

Preheat oven to 325F (165C). Beat the eggs in a medium bowl until lemon colored. Beat in the sugar, salt, and pepper. Stir in the corn, onion, and milk. Place each well-drained tomato, cut side up, in a greased 6-ounce glass baking cup. Fill each tomato shell with the corn mixture.

Bake 45 to 55 minutes, or just until a knife inserted off-center in filling comes out clean. Top each tomato with cheese and chopped parsley.

Corn, Bean, & Tomato Bowl

MAKES ABOUT 4 TO 6 SERVINGS

Take this dish to your next picnic or pot luck; top with the corn chips at the last minute.

1 (10- to 12-oz.) can whole-kernel corn, drained

1 (15- to 16-oz.) can black beans, drained

1 small cucumber, peeled and diced

3 medium-size tomatoes, coarsely chopped

2 green onions, chopped

¼ cup vegetable oil

2 tablespoons red wine vinegar

1 teaspoon Worcestershire sauce

2 tablespoons ketchup

1 tablespoon honey

1 tablespoon prepared mustard

1 teaspoon soy sauce

½ cup coarsely crumbled corn chips

Combine the corn, beans, cucumber, tomatoes, and onions in a large bowl.

Whisk together the oil, vinegar, Worcestershire sauce, ketchup, honey, mustard, and soy sauce in a small bowl. Pour the dressing over the vegetable mixture; toss to combine. Sprinkle with the crumbled corn chips just before serving.

Comfort Foods

These are the home-style dishes that transport you to your

grandmother's house, whether her origins are from Italy, the

Caribbean, or the Deep South, when you take the first spoonful.

They provide recollections of the sweet memories of childhood.

Warm and friendly, they give you a safe comfortable feeling.

Meatloaf, tuna casserole, chicken pot pie, and brisket have all been

updated but still retain their nostalgic, home-cooked feel. For

example, Smoked Albacore Tetrazzini is an upscale tuna casserole,

and Chicken Pot Pie has surprises under the crust that enhance its

old-fashioned flavor and aroma.

Spicy Brisket with Potatoes

Chicken, Cabbage, & Apple Bake

Chicken Pot Pie

Dijon Turkey with Orzo

Hoppin' John

Upside Down Meatloaf with Jasmine Rice

Pork Strips with Potatoes & Cabbage

Smoked Albacore Tetrazzini

Turkey Cornbread Wedges

Beef, Black Bean, & Sweet Potato Casserole

Polenta & Sausage Bake

Chicken & Sausage Jambalaya

Bacon, Cheese, & Tomato Pasta Bake

Deep-Dish Pizza

Spicy Brisket with Potatoes

MAKES 6 TO 8 SERVINGS

Beer not only adds a subtle flavor but also aids in tenderizing the beef. Serve with coleslaw made from a shredded cabbage mix.

- 1 tablespoon vegetable oil
- 1 (2- to 3-pound) beef brisket
- ½ teaspoon salt
- ¼ teaspoon freshly ground pepper
- 2 leeks, sliced
- 1 (12-oz.) bottle or can of beer
- ½ cup water
- 1 tablespoon light brown sugar
- 2 tablespoons spicy brown mustard
- 1 tablespoon prepared horseradish
- 2 teaspoons beef bouillon granules
- 1 pound baby red potatoes, cut in half

Heat the oil in a 4-quart Dutch oven or pan over medium heat. Add the brisket; cook until brown. Turn and brown the other side. Sprinkle with the salt and pepper. Stir in the leeks, then the beer, water, brown sugar, mustard, horseradish, and bouillon granules.

Cover and cook, over low heat until the beef is almost tender, 3 hours. Add the potatoes and cook, covered, until the beef and potatoes are tender, 25 to 30 minutes.

Chicken, Cabbage, & Apple Bake

MAKES 4 OR 5 SERVINGS

Savoy cabbage's crinkled green leaves form a round head. It can be found year-round in any supermarket.

1 (3½-pound) frying chicken, cut into pieces

1 tablespoon vegetable oil

½ head savoy cabbage, shredded

1 small onion, sliced

½ teaspoon salt

2 apples, cored and cut into wedges

3 tablespoons soy sauce

2 tablespoons grated fresh ginger

⅛ teaspoon crushed red pepper flakes

1 tablespoon honey

Rinse and pat dry the chicken pieces. Heat the oil in a 4-quart Dutch oven or electric skillet over medium heat. Brown the chicken on all sides. Remove from pan.

Place the cabbage in bottom of the pan. Add the onion and salt and top with chicken and apples. Combine the soy sauce, ginger, pepper flakes, and honey. Spoon over the chicken and apples.

Cover and cook over medium-low heat about 50 minutes, or until chicken is tender.

Chicken Pot Pie

MAKES 6 TO 8 SERVINGS

Recall the past with this updated classic.

1 large fennel bulb

2 tablespoons vegetable oil

1 cup baby carrots

4 medium yellow pattypan squash, each cut into 12 wedges

1 cup quartered small crimini mushrooms

1 (6½-oz.) jar artichoke hearts in water, drained and sliced

3 cups coarsely chopped cooked chicken

3 tablespoons all-purpose flour

1 (14½-oz.) can chicken broth

1 cup half-and-half

2 cups buttermilk baking mix

1 cup milk

1 egg, lightly beaten

Thinly slice the fennel bulb, reserving the leafy tops. Chop leafy tops and set aside.

Heat the oil in a large skillet over medium heat. Add the sliced fennel and carrots. Cook, stirring occasionally, about 5 minutes. Stir in the squash and cook 8 minutes. Add the mushrooms, artichokes, and chicken. Sprinkle the flour over contents of skillet. Stir well; add the broth and half-and-half. Cook, stirring occasionally, until thickened and bubbly.

Transfer chicken mixture to a 13 × 9-inch baking dish. Preheat oven to 375F (190C). In a medium bowl, beat together the baking mix, milk, egg, and 1 tablespoon of the chopped fennel leaves until combined. Pour over chicken mixture in dish.

Bake 25 minutes, or until crust is brown.

Dijon Turkey with Orzo

MAKES ABOUT 4 SERVINGS

Orzo looks like rice, but it is a type of pasta. If orzo is not available, substitute another very small pasta shape or even rice.

¾ cup uncooked orzo or riso pasta

¼ cup butter or margarine

1 (¾- to 1-pound) turkey breast, cut into 2 × ½-inch strips

2 shallots, minced

3 zucchini, shredded

⅓ cup Dijon mustard

1 tablespoon fresh lemon juice

2 tablespoons white wine

¼ teaspoon salt

¼ teaspoon freshly ground black pepper

1½ cups mini tomatoes (see Note, page 36)

2 tablespoons chopped fresh parsley

½ cup freshly grated Romano cheese

Cook the orzo according to package directions; drain and set aside.

Melt the butter in a large skillet over medium heat. Stir in the turkey, shallots, zucchini, mustard, lemon juice, wine, salt, and pepper. Cook, stirring occasionally, until turkey is no longer pink, 5 to 10 minutes. Stir in the orzo and tomatoes. Sprinkle with parsley and cheese. Toss to coat. Serve hot.

Hoppin' John

MAKES 4 SERVINGS

It's a southern tradition to eat black-eyed peas on New Year's Day so you will have good luck all year.

11 ounces fresh or frozen shelled black-eyed peas

6 slices bacon, chopped

1 large onion, chopped

1 stalk celery, finely chopped

2 (14½-oz.) cans chicken broth

1 cup uncooked long-grain white rice

¼ teaspoon freshly ground black pepper

¼ cup chopped fresh parsley

Cook the peas according to package directions. Drain and set aside. Cook the bacon in a 4-quart Dutch oven or electric skillet on medium heat until almost crisp. Drain off the fat, reserving bacon and 2 tablespoons of the fat.

Return the reserved fat to the pan. Stir in the onion and celery. Cook until softened, about 5 minutes. Add the chicken broth, rice, and pepper. Bring to a boil. Cover and reduce heat to low. Cook until rice is tender, 20 to 25 minutes.

Stir in the peas and reserved bacon. Sprinkle with parsley and serve.

Upside Down Meatloaf with Jasmine Rice

MAKES 4 TO 6 SERVINGS

Named after the fragrant jasmine flower, jasmine rice is a type of long-grain white rice with a wonderful aroma and flavor.

1 cup pitted whole ripe olives

1 cup uncooked white jasmine rice

2 cups boiling water

1½ pounds lean ground beef TRX TURKEY!

1 small onion, minced

2 cloves garlic, minced

¼ cup pine nuts

¼ teaspoon ground cumin

⅛ teaspoon ground allspice

⅛ teaspoon ground cloves

½ teaspoon salt

¼ teaspoon freshly ground black pepper

2 tablespoons vegetable oil

2 small Japanese eggplant or 1 small regular eggplant, cut into ¼-inch-diagonal slices

1 (14½-oz.) can beef broth

Preheat oven to 350F (175C). Grease a 2½- to 3-quart round or oval baking dish. Arrange olives over bottom of prepared dish; set aside. In a medium bowl, cover rice with boiling water. Let stand 5 minutes. Drain, discarding water. Set rice aside. In a large bowl, combine the beef, onion, garlic, nuts, cumin, allspice, cloves, salt, and pepper. Press the beef mixture in the baking dish, covering the bottom completely. Spread the rice over the beef mixture.

Heat the oil in a skillet over medium-high heat. Add the eggplant and brown on both sides. Arrange the eggplant on the baking dish. Pour broth over all. Cover tightly.

Bake 50 to 60 minutes, or until rice is tender. Let stand, covered, 5 minutes. Loosen edges around pan. Invert onto large heat-proof serving platter. Cut into slices and serve.

Pork Strips with Potatoes & Cabbage

MAKES 4 OR 5 SERVINGS

Potatoes, cabbage, and stewed tomatoes. How much more down-home can you get?

1 tablespoon vegetable oil

1 ¼ pounds boneless pork strips

1 onion, chopped

1 (14½-oz.) can sliced stewed tomatoes

½ small head cabbage, coarsely shredded

½ teaspoon salt

⅛ teaspoon freshly ground black pepper

1 teaspoon caraway seeds

1 teaspoon honey

4 medium potatoes, peeled and quartered

Heat the oil in a 4-quart Dutch oven or an electric skillet over medium heat. Add the pork; brown on all sides. Stir in the onion, tomatoes, cabbage, salt, pepper, caraway seeds, and honey.

Cover and simmer, stirring occasionally, about 45 minutes. Add the potatoes, cook, covered, until pork and vegetables are tender, about 30 minutes.

Smoked Albacore Tetrazzini

MAKES 4 TO 6 SERVINGS

Mizithra is a Greek hard cheese made from sheep's milk. Romano cheese is a good substitute.

¼ cup butter or margarine

¼ cup all-purpose flour

1 (14½-oz.) can chicken broth

1 cup half-and-half

1 cup sliced fresh mushrooms

1 (13¾-oz.) can quartered artichoke hearts in water, drained

¼ teaspoon salt

⅛ teaspoon freshly ground black pepper

⅛ teaspoon ground nutmeg

2 tablespoons white wine

8 ounces uncooked linguine or fettuccini

8 ounces smoked albacore or yellowfin tuna, coarsely chopped

⅔ cup freshly grated mizithra or Romano cheese

⅓ cup freshly grated Parmesan cheese

Melt the butter in a medium saucepan over medium heat. Stir in the flour; cook, stirring, until bubbly, 2 to 3 minutes. Add the broth, half-and-half, mushrooms, artichokes, salt, pepper, nutmeg, and wine. Bring to a boil; reduce heat and simmer 2 to 3 minutes, stirring often.

Preheat oven to 350F (175C). Grease an 11 × 7-inch baking dish. Cook the pasta according to package directions; drain. Combine the pasta, tuna, sauce, and mizithra cheese. Spoon into prepared dish. Sprinkle with the Parmesan cheese.

Bake 20 to 30 minutes, or until bubbly. Serve hot.

Turkey Cornbread Wedges

MAKES 6 SERVINGS

Buy the cornbread from a bakery to cut preparation time.

1 (13-oz.) package cornbread mix

1 tablespoon vegetable oil

1 (1-pound) package turkey breast strips

1 clove garlic, minced

1 (16-oz.) jar picante sauce

Kernels from 2 ears of corn (about 1 cup)

½ cup sliced ripe green olives

2 green onions, sliced

2 teaspoons unsweetened cocoa powder

1 teaspoon ground cumin

1 cup (4 ounces) shredded Colby-Jack cheese

⅓ cup sour cream

1 tablespoon finely chopped fresh cilantro

Grease a 9-inch-round baking pan. Prepare cornbread mix according to package directions. Bake in prepared pan. Cut into 6 wedges; set aside.

Heat the oil in a large skillet over medium-high heat. Add the turkey and garlic; cook, stirring, until turkey is no longer pink. Measure ½ cup of the picante sauce; set aside. Stir the remaining picante sauce, corn, olives, onions, cocoa powder, and cumin into turkey mixture. Cook, stirring, over medium heat until turkey is tender, about 10 minutes.

Split each cornbread wedge in half horizontally. Place bottom halves on individual plates. Spoon half of the turkey mixture over bottom wedges. Cover with the cornbread tops and remaining turkey mixture. Top with cheese, sour cream, and cilantro. Pass reserved picante sauce.

Beef, Black Bean, & Sweet Potato Casserole

MAKES 4 TO 6 SERVINGS

If you're longing for a taste of the Caribbean, this island-style dish with a touch of spice and sweetness will satisfy your craving.

1 pound lean ground beef

1 (8-oz.) can tomato sauce

1 tablespoon chili powder

1 teaspoon ground cumin

½ teaspoon salt

1 (15-oz.) can black beans, drained

2 medium sweet potatoes, peeled and thinly sliced

⅓ cup chopped raisins

2 plum tomatoes, chopped

1 large mild green chile, seeded and chopped

1 small onion, chopped

1 cup (4 ounces) shredded Cheddar cheese

Preheat oven to 350F (175C). Grease a 2½- or 3-quart baking dish. Brown the beef in a medium skillet over medium heat until no longer pink, stirring to break up. Drain and discard any fat. Stir in the tomato sauce, chili powder, cumin, and salt.

Spread the beans in an even layer in prepared dish. Layer the potatoes over the beans. Sprinkle with the raisins, tomatoes, chile, and onion. Spread the beef mixture over the vegetables.

Cover and bake 45 minutes. Uncover; top with the cheese and bake 15 minutes, or until potatoes are done. Serve hot.

Polenta & Sausage Bake

MAKES 4 SERVINGS

Creamy polenta with a buttery cheese topping makes a satisfying meal.

1½ **cups yellow cornmeal**

2 (14½-oz.) **cans chicken broth**

¼ **cup butter or margarine, chilled**

¾ **cup freshly grated Romano cheese**

½ **pound bulk sweet Italian turkey sausage**

3 **tomatoes, peeled, seeded, and chopped**

2 **zucchini, coarsely shredded**

2 **cloves garlic, minced**

Combine the cornmeal and broth in medium saucepan over medium heat. Bring to a boil, stirring occasionally; reduce heat to medium-low. Cook, stirring constantly, until thickened and bubbly, 10 minutes. Rinse a 15 × 10-inch pan with cold water. Spread cornmeal mixture in pan; refrigerate, uncovered, until firm, about 30 minutes.

Cut the butter into the cheese in a medium bowl; refrigerate until needed. Brown the sausage in large skillet over medium heat, stirring to break up. Add the tomatoes, zucchini, and garlic. Cook over medium-high heat 10 minutes; set aside.

Preheat oven to 350F (175C). Grease an 11 × 7-inch baking dish. Cut the cold cornmeal into 3 × 2-inch strips.

Arrange one third of the strips in the prepared pan. Layer half of the meat sauce over the strips. Sprinkle with one third of the cheese-butter mixture. Repeat layers, ending with the cheese-butter mixture on top.

Bake 30 to 40 minutes, or until bubbly. Let stand 5 minutes before serving.

Chicken & Sausage Jambalaya

MAKES ABOUT 6 SERVINGS

This jambalaya will be spicy. If you prefer it milder, reduce the cayenne pepper.

2 tablespoons butter or margarine

6 boneless, skinless chicken thighs, cut into 1-inch cubes

8 ounces andouille sausage, halved lengthwise and cut into ½-inch-thick slices

1 large onion, chopped

2 stalks celery, chopped

1 large poblano chile, seeded and chopped (see Note, page 71)

2 cloves garlic, minced

2 tomatoes, peeled, seeded, and chopped

1 (8-oz.) can tomato sauce

½ teaspoon cayenne pepper

½ teaspoon freshly ground black pepper

1 teaspoon dried oregano

1 teaspoon dried thyme

2 (14½-oz.) cans chicken broth

1 cup uncooked long-grain white rice

Melt the butter in a 4- to 6-quart saucepan over medium-high heat. Add the chicken and sausage. Cook, stirring occasionally, until the meat begins to brown. Stir in the vegetables; cook until softened, about 10 minutes. Add the tomato sauce, cayenne and black peppers, oregano, thyme, and chicken broth. Cover and cook over low heat 30 minutes.

Stir in the rice. Bring to a boil. Reduce heat; cover and cook over low heat about 30 minutes, or until rice is tender.

Bacon, Cheese, & Tomato Pasta Bake

MAKES 5 OR 6 SERVINGS

The combination of flavors will remind you of your favorite grilled cheese, bacon, and tomato sandwich. A dry white wine goes well with this dish.

8 ounces uncooked medium pasta shells

3 bacon slices, chopped

2 tablespoons all-purpose flour

1 cup milk

¼ teaspoon salt

⅛ teaspoon freshly ground black pepper

2 large tomatoes, coarsely chopped

1 cup (4 ounces) shredded Cheddar cheese

Preheat oven to 350F (175C). Grease a 2-quart baking dish.

Cook the pasta according to package directions; drain and set aside.

While the pasta cooks, cook the bacon in a large skillet until crisp; remove with a slotted spoon. Stir the flour into the fat in the skillet. Gradually stir in the milk, salt, and pepper; cook, stirring, until thickened.

Spoon half of the cooked pasta into the prepared dish. Add half of the bacon and sauce, then half of the tomatoes. Repeat the layers. Top with the cheese.

Bake, uncovered, about 20 minutes, or until cheese melts and mixture is bubbly.

VARIATION
The recipe can be doubled for a large party. Bake in a 13 × 9-inch baking dish.

Deep-Dish Pizza

MAKES 6 SERVINGS

The crust of this version is slightly thicker than traditional pizza; it has a biscuit-like texture.

1 cup all-purpose flour

1½ teaspoons baking powder

½ teaspoon salt

¼ cup butter or margarine, chilled

1 large egg, slightly beaten

½ cup milk

1½ tablespoons cornmeal

1½ cups (6 ounces) shredded mozzarella cheese

16 to 18 thin pepperoni slices

1 cup sliced fresh mushrooms

½ cup diced green bell pepper

1 (14-oz.) jar pizza sauce (1½ to 1⅔ cups)

¼ cup freshly grated Parmesan cheese

Preheat oven to 425F (220C). Combine the flour, baking powder, and salt in a medium bowl. Cut in the butter until the mixture resembles cornmeal. Stir in the egg and milk to form a thick batter.

Lightly oil a 9-inch-round baking pan. Sprinkle with the cornmeal, coating the bottom and side of the pan. Spread the batter evenly over the bottom of the pan. Sprinkle the mozzarella cheese over the batter. Top with the pepperoni, mushrooms, and bell pepper. Spoon the pizza sauce over all. Sprinkle with the Parmesan cheese.

Bake 20 to 25 minutes or until brown and bubbly. Let stand 5 to 10 minutes; cut into wedges and serve.

Meal-in-a-Bowl Salads

On a hot summer day, a salad that satisfies is a welcome light

evening meal or lunch. These cool favorites combine classic

ingredients updated with today's popular foods. Impress guests

with Italian Seashell Plates. These individual salads are

sophisticated and tasty. Margarita Rice Salad is a bowl full of fun

and flavor. The rice is first cooked in pineapple-orange juice, then

tossed with a dressing of tequila and fruit juices.

Be sure to try it at your next fiesta.

Fried Chicken Salad

Ham & Cheese Pasta Toss

Italian Seashell Plate

Margarita Rice Salad

Layered Tomato-Rice Salad

Reuben Salad Bowl

Salad Bowl Dinner

Smoked Turkey, Melon, & Orange Bowl

Summertime Special

Multilayered Salad Toss

Tortellini Vegetable Combo

Wild West Toss

Venetian Shrimp Bowl

Fried Chicken Salad

MAKES 4 SERVINGS

An all-American diner favorite, this salad can easily be made at home.

6 to 8 cups torn iceberg or romaine lettuce

2 green onions, sliced

1 large tomato, chopped

4 strips bacon, crisp-cooked and crumbled

3 hard-cooked eggs, chopped

1 cup (4 ounces) shredded Cheddar cheese

1 (10-oz.) package frozen breaded boneless chicken pieces

3 tablespoons honey

¼ cup Dijon mustard

3 tablespoons white wine vinegar

⅔ cup vegetable oil

½ teaspoon salt

¼ teaspoon freshly ground black pepper

Dash hot pepper sauce

Place the lettuce in a large serving bowl. Add the onions, tomato, bacon, eggs, and cheese.

Heat the chicken according to package directions. Let cool slightly.

Whisk together the honey, mustard, vinegar, oil, salt, pepper, and hot pepper sauce in a small bowl. Drizzle dressing over salad. Add chicken; toss to combine. Serve immediately.

Ham & Cheese Pasta Toss

MAKES 4 TO 6 SERVINGS

Orzo is a pasta shaped like rice.

6 ounces (¾ cup) uncooked orzo

2 tablespoons sweet-hot mustard

2 tablespoons white wine vinegar

¼ cup vegetable oil

¼ teaspoon crushed red pepper flakes

8 ounces cooked lean ham, cut into small strips (2 cups)

1 small jicama, peeled and cut into small strips

1 medium carrot, peeled and coarsely shredded

1 small red onion, thinly sliced

4 ounces Gruyère cheese, cut into small strips (1 cup)

Cook the pasta according to package directions; drain and cool. Combine the mustard and vinegar in a small bowl; stir in the oil and pepper flakes; set aside.

Combine the pasta, ham, jicama, carrot, onion, and cheese in a large bowl. Pour dressing over the salad; toss to combine.

Italian Seashell Plate

MAKES 4 OR 5 SERVINGS

Let your artistic inspiration take over to create these elegant individual salads.

8 ounces medium pasta shells

8 anchovies, finely chopped

⅓ cup olive oil

3 tablespoons balsamic vinegar

1 clove garlic, minced

2 tablespoons chopped fresh parsley

⅛ teaspoon freshly ground black pepper

8 to 10 lettuce or endive leaves

8 to 10 cherry tomatoes, halved

1 (6-oz.) jar marinated artichoke hearts, drained and quartered

3 hard-cooked eggs, peeled and quartered

¼ cup sliced ripe olives

Cook the pasta according to package directions; drain and cool.

Whisk together the anchovies, oil, vinegar, garlic, parsley, and pepper. Pour over pasta; toss to coat.

Line individual plates with the lettuce. Top with the dressed pasta. Arrange the cherry tomatoes, artichokes, and eggs around the pasta. Garnish with the olives.

Margarita Rice Salad

MAKES 6 TO 8 SERVINGS

If you prefer not to use the tequila in the dressing, you can use 1 tablespoon more lime juice instead.

- 1 cup pineapple-orange juice
- 2 cups chicken broth
- 1½ cups uncooked long-grain white rice
- ¾ pound boneless turkey breast, cut into 2 × ½-inch strips
- 1 (1-oz.) package dry ranch salad dressing mix
- 1 tablespoon vegetable oil
- 1 small poblano or mild green chile, seeded and chopped
- 1 (11-oz.) can white and yellow corn, drained
- 1 (15-oz.) can red beans, drained

TEQUILA DRESSING

- ¼ cup pineapple-orange juice
- ⅓ cup vegetable oil
- ¼ cup plain yogurt
- 2 tablespoons fresh lime juice
- 1 tablespoon tequila
- 2 teaspoons sugar
- ½ teaspoon salt
- ½ teaspoon ground cumin
- 1 cup loosely packed cilantro leaves

Bring 1 cup of juice and the broth to a boil in a medium saucepan. Stir in the rice. Cover and cook over low heat until tender, about 20 minutes; set aside.

Coat the turkey with the dry salad dressing mix. Heat the oil in a medium skillet over medium heat. Add the turkey and chile. Cook, stirring over medium heat, until turkey is cooked through; remove from heat.

Make the dressing: In a blender or food processor, combine all the dressing ingredients. Process until very finely chopped.

Thoroughly mix the rice, turkey, corn, beans, and dressing in a large bowl. Serve warm or cold.

Layered Tomato-Rice Salad

MAKES 4 OR 5 SERVINGS

This beautifully layered salad makes an impressive presentation. The seasoned rice and other ingredients give it the flavors of a California roll, but it is much easier to do.

3 to 4 tomatoes, very thinly sliced

1 cup uncooked medium-grain white rice

3 tablespoons seasoned rice vinegar

2 tablespoons soy sauce

1 tablespoon grated fresh ginger

1 teaspoon sugar

2 tablespoons chopped fresh chives

2 Japanese cucumbers or 1 English cucumber, peeled and coarsely shredded (see Note, page 75)

1 (3-oz.) package thinly sliced smoked salmon

Line a 2- to 2½-quart bowl with plastic wrap, overlapping and leaving about 6 inches overhanging top of bowl. Place about half of the tomato slices on bottom and up sides, using the best ones.

Cook the rice according to package directions. While still hot, stir in the vinegar, soy sauce, ginger, and sugar. Cool to lukewarm. Press half of the rice firmly into bottom of lined bowl over the tomatoes. Sprinkle with the chives. Spread the cucumber in an even layer over the rice. Layer half of the salmon over the cucumber. Place a layer of tomato slices over the salmon. Press the remaining rice in an even layer. Top with the remaining salmon, and tomatoes.

Cover with the overhanging plastic wrap and use a weighted plate to compress the salad. Refrigerate overnight. To serve, fold plastic wrap back, place a plate on the bowl, and invert the salad onto the plate. Remove the plastic wrap and cut into wedges.

Reuben Salad Bowl

MAKES 4 SERVINGS.

Instead of making a Reuben sandwich with leftover corned beef, try this flavorful salad.

    8 ounces cooked corned beef

    1 (8-oz.) can sauerkraut, drained

    1 small red onion, sliced

    1 (14- to 15-oz.) can small white potatoes, drained

    4 ounces sliced Swiss cheese, cut into 1-inch strips

    ½ cup mayonnaise

    1 teaspoon Dijon mustard

    2 tablespoons Heinz chili sauce

    ¼ teaspoon caraway seeds

Cut the corned beef into ¼-inch-thick slices, then into 2-inch-wide strips.

Combine the corned beef, sauerkraut, onion, potatoes, and cheese in a large salad bowl.

Combine the mayonnaise, mustard, chili sauce, and caraway seeds in a small bowl. Pour over corned beef mixture; toss until well blended.

Salad Bowl Dinner

MAKES 4 TO 6 SERVINGS

Leek soup mix creates an easy dressing for this mouthwatering salad.

1 (1.8-oz.) package dry leek soup mix

½ cup sour cream

½ cup plain nonfat or regular yogurt

4 cups shredded iceberg lettuce

2 cups diced cooked turkey or chicken

2 green onions, chopped

2 tomatoes, chopped

1 cup cooked corn or 1 (8-oz.) can whole-kernel corn, drained

¼ cup chopped peanuts

Combine the dry leek soup mix, sour cream, and yogurt in a medium bowl; set aside.

Combine the lettuce, turkey, onions, tomatoes, and corn in a large bowl. Add the dressing; toss until well blended. Sprinkle with the peanuts.

Smoked Turkey, Melon, & Orange Bowl

MAKES 4 SERVINGS

A summer treat that requires no cooking, it takes advantage of the many new cooked turkey products that are available.

8 ounces boneless, skinless smoked cooked turkey, cut in julienned slices

½ small honeydew melon, peeled and cubed

1 (11-oz.) can mandarin oranges, drained

2 cups chopped endive leaves

2 to 3 cups coarsely chopped butter lettuce

1 cup snow peas, cut in half

DRESSING

¼ cup vegetable oil

1 clove garlic, minced

1 tablespoon minced crystallized ginger

1 tablespoon toasted sesame seeds

2 tablespoons soy sauce

2 tablespoons seasoned rice vinegar

1 teaspoon honey

Combine the turkey, melon, oranges, endive, lettuce, and snow peas in a large bowl.

Prepare the dressing: Combine all the ingredients in a small bowl. Pour dressing over salad; toss to combine. Serve immediately.

Summertime Special

MAKES ABOUT 6 SERVINGS

Use fresh ears of corn whenever available for the freshest flavor.

Kernels from 2 ears of corn or 1 (10-oz.) package frozen corn

1 (15- to 16-oz.) can pinto beans, drained

2 large tomatoes, coarsely chopped

2 green onions, chopped

1 medium cucumber, peeled and diced

⅓ pound cooked ham, cut into strips (about 1 cup)

¼ cup vegetable oil

2 tablespoons red wine vinegar

1 tablespoon Worcestershire sauce

2 tablespoons ketchup

1 tablespoon honey

1 tablespoon prepared mustard

1 tablespoon soy sauce

½ cup crumbled corn chips

Cook the corn in boiling water about 3 minutes; drain. Combine the corn, beans, tomatoes, onions, cucumber, and ham in a large bowl.

Whisk the oil, vinegar, Worcestershire sauce, ketchup, honey, mustard, and soy sauce until blended in a small bowl. Pour over vegetables and ham. Toss until combined.

Sprinkle the salad with crumbled corn chips just before serving. Use a slotted spoon to serve, discarding any liquid.

Multilayered Salad Toss

MAKES 4 TO 6 SERVINGS

This salad is so attractive that you will want to use your prettiest glass bowl to show it off.

2 medium tomatoes, peeled and cubed

1 cup small cubes Monterey Jack cheese

4 slices (about 3 ounces) cooked ham, julienned

1 (15- or 16-oz.) can small red beans, drained

2 green onions, sliced

1 small yellow or red bell pepper, julienned

3 cups shredded lettuce or mixed greens

⅓ cup olive oil

¼ cup white wine vinegar

1 clove garlic, crushed

1 tablespoon finely chopped fresh cilantro

½ teaspoon salt

⅛ teaspoon freshly ground black pepper

1 avocado or sliced ripe olives

Make layers of the tomatoes, cheese, ham, beans, onions, bell pepper, and lettuce in a 2½-quart glass salad bowl, starting with tomatoes and ending with lettuce. Serve at once or cover and refrigerate up to 3 hours.

Whisk together the oil, vinegar, garlic, cilantro, salt, and black pepper in a small bowl. Pour the dressing over the layered salad; toss to combine. Peel, pit, and slice the avocado. Garnish the salad with avocado slices.

Tortellini Vegetable Combo

MAKES 4 TO 5 SERVINGS

Gently pull a vegetable peeler across the surface of a chunk of Parmesan cheese to make slightly curled shavings.

1 (8- to 9-oz.) package uncooked fresh or frozen chicken and prosciutto tortellini

1 (16-oz.) package frozen mixed vegetables

1 cup cherry tomatoes, halved (about 12 tomatoes)

⅓ cup vegetable oil

2 tablespoons white wine vinegar

1 teaspoon fresh lemon juice

1 tablespoon Dijon mustard

¼ teaspoon salt

⅛ teaspoon freshly ground black pepper

¼ cup thinly shaved Parmesan cheese

Cook the tortellini and frozen vegetables according to package directions; drain. Cool the tortellini and vegetables; combine with the tomatoes in a large bowl.

Whisk together the oil, vinegar, lemon juice, mustard, salt, and pepper in a small bowl. Pour the dressing over the vegetable mixture; toss to combine. Top salad with shaved cheese.

Wild West Toss

MAKES ABOUT 4 SERVINGS

An attractive, colorful salad, it can be made ahead for a picnic or barbecue.

- 3 medium tomatoes, chopped
- 1 small red onion, chopped
- 1 small yellow or green bell pepper, chopped
- 1 (28-oz.) can pinto beans, drained
- 1 cup diced cooked ham (about 5 ounces)
- 1 tablespoon chopped fresh basil
- 2 tablespoons vegetable oil
- 2 tablespoons red wine vinegar
- ½ teaspoon chili powder
- ¼ teaspoon salt
- ⅛ teaspoon freshly ground black pepper
- 2 tablespoons freshly grated Parmesan cheese

Combine the tomatoes, onion, bell pepper, beans, ham, and basil in a large bowl.

Whisk together the oil, vinegar, chili powder, salt, and black pepper in a small bowl. Pour the dressing over bean mixture; toss to combine. Sprinkle the cheese over the salad.

Venetian Shrimp Bowl

MAKES 4 TO 6 SERVINGS

This delicious combination of shrimp and cannellini beans makes a salad that's hearty enough to be featured as a main dish.

12 ounces cooked shelled medium shrimp, halved lengthwise

1 (16-oz.) can cannellini beans, drained

4 large plum tomatoes, cut into thin wedges

2 green onions, sliced

1 tablespoon chopped fresh basil

¼ cup olive oil

2 tablespoons fresh lemon juice

1 tablespoon Dijon mustard

1 clove garlic, crushed

¼ teaspoon salt

⅛ teaspoon freshly ground black pepper

Ripe olives

Combine the shrimp, beans, tomatoes, onions, and basil in a large bowl.

Whisk together the oil, lemon juice, mustard, garlic, salt, and pepper in a small bowl. Pour the dressing over the shrimp mixture; toss until well coated. Garnish with the olives.

Soups, Chilies, & Stews

Meals that include soups always feel comfortable and nostalgic.

They return us to the past with each satisfying bite. Meal-in-a-

Bowl Minestrone is a vegetable soup enhanced by the addition

of the richly flavored Italian ham, proscuitto. Or try one

of the chilies; you're sure to find a favorite.

Italian Flavors Soup

Sausage Bean Soup

Farm-Style Corn Chowder

Short Rib Stew

Speedy Posole

Black Bean Chili with Goat Cheese

Gringo Chili

Pinto Turkey Chili

Corn 'n' Bean Chili

Fresh Tomato Chili

Green Chile Stew

Southwestern Cheese Soup

Portuguese Red Bean Soup

Mediterranean Fish Stew

Turkey Stew & Rice

Border Town Bean Soup

Fennel, Leek, & Potato Soup

Meal-in-a-Bowl Minestrone

Curried Carrot Soup

Fresh Corn Soup

Italian Flavors Soup

MAKES 4 OR 5 SERVINGS

A hearty soup that's produced in minutes, yet has traditional old-fashioned Italian flavors.

1 tablespoon vegetable oil

8 slices salami, cut into thin strips (about 1 ½ ounces)

2 cups shredded cabbage

1 (8-oz.) can garbanzo beans, drained

1 (15- to 16-oz.) can diced peeled tomatoes in tomato juice

2 cups beef broth or bouillon

½ teaspoon dried Italian seasoning, crumbled

¼ teaspoon salt

⅛ teaspoon freshly ground black pepper

Heat the oil in a 2-quart pan. Add the salami; cook, stirring, over medium heat 2 or 3 minutes.

Stir in the cabbage, beans, tomatoes, broth, seasoning, salt, and pepper. Cover and simmer about 8 minutes, or until cabbage is tender.

Sausage Bean Soup

MAKES 6 TO 8 SERVINGS

If you are hesitant about trying spicy foods, omit the hot pepper sauce or start with a few drops and taste before adding more.

1 (12-oz.) package Portuguese or hot Italian sausage

2 ham hocks

1 medium onion, chopped

1 medium carrot, chopped

2 celery stalks, chopped

2 medium tomatoes, chopped

2 (8-oz.) cans tomato sauce

2 cups water

½ teaspoon salt

⅛ teaspoon freshly ground black pepper

2 or 3 dashes hot pepper sauce

2 cups coarsely shredded cabbage

2 (16-oz.) cans dried lima beans (butter beans), drained

Sauté the sausage in a 4-quart saucepan until brown, about 5 minutes, stirring to break up. Drain off fat.

Add the ham hocks, onion, carrot, celery, tomatoes, tomato sauce, water, salt, pepper, and hot sauce. Cover and simmer 2 hours.

Remove the ham hocks; discard bone, skin, and fat. Cube the meat and return to pot. Add the cabbage and beans; cook about 30 minutes, or until cabbage is tender.

Farm-Style Corn Chowder

MAKES ABOUT 6 SERVINGS

This hearty chowder is filling enough to be used as a main dish.

- 1 onion, finely chopped
- 6 to 8 ounces smoky sausage links, sliced
- 1 potato, finely chopped
- 2 cups chicken broth or bouillon
- 1 (16-oz.) can cream-style corn
- ¼ cup canned diced green chiles
- 2 medium tomatoes, chopped
- ¼ teaspoon salt
- ¼ teaspoon garlic salt

Combine the onion, sausage, potato, and broth in a 2-quart saucepan. Cover and simmer over low heat 15 minutes.

Stir in the corn, chiles, tomatoes, salt, and garlic salt. Cover; simmer 4 or 5 minutes to allow flavors to blend.

Short Rib Stew

MAKES 5 OR 6 SERVINGS

Choose extra-lean short ribs; if they are not available, carefully brown the ribs on all sides and pour off the fat before adding other ingredients.

> 2½ to 3 pounds lean short ribs
>
> 2 leeks, cut into ½-inch slices
>
> 4 carrots, cut into ½-inch pieces
>
> 4 new potatoes, quartered
>
> 4 plum tomatoes, quartered
>
> ½ teaspoon dried leaf marjoram
>
> 1 teaspoon Worcestershire sauce
>
> ½ teaspoon salt
>
> ⅛ teaspoon freshly ground black pepper
>
> 2 cups beef broth or bouillon
>
> ¼ cup cornstarch
>
> ¼ cup cold water

Heat a large Dutch oven over medium heat. Add the short ribs; brown on all sides. Pour off fat.

Add the leeks, carrots, potatoes, tomatoes, marjoram, Worcestershire sauce, salt, pepper, and broth. Cook, covered, 2 hours, or until tender.

Dissolve the cornstarch in the water; stir into hot stew. Cook over low heat, stirring constantly, until thickened.

Speedy Posole

MAKES ABOUT 6 SERVINGS

Large soup bowls are ideal for serving this dish because it has quite a bit of wonderful broth; yet it is much heartier than most soups.

1 pound lean boneless pork, cut into ½-inch cubes

1 (4-oz.) can diced green chiles, drained

1 small onion, chopped

1 (15- or 16-oz.) can diced tomatoes in tomato juice

1 clove garlic, crushed

1 teaspoon chili powder

½ teaspoon salt

2 cups chicken broth or bouillon

1 (29-oz.) can white or yellow hominy, drained

1 tablespoon chopped fresh cilantro

¼ cup sour cream or plain yogurt

Combine the pork cubes, chiles, onion, tomatoes, garlic, chili powder, salt, broth, and hominy in a 4-quart pan. Cover and simmer 30 to 35 minutes, or until pork is tender.

Add the cilantro; spoon into large individual soup bowls. Top each bowl with sour cream.

Black Bean Chili with Goat Cheese

MAKES 6 TO 8 SERVINGS

Puree one can of the beans and use the other one as is for a slightly thickened soup with lots of texture.

- 1 tablespoon vegetable or olive oil
- 1 medium onion, chopped
- 1 yellow or green bell pepper, chopped
- 1 clove garlic, crushed
- 1 jalapeño chile, seeded and chopped
- 1 (28-oz.) can chopped tomatoes
- 1 teaspoon chili powder
- ½ teaspoon sweet paprika
- ½ teaspoon salt
- ½ teaspoon dried oregano leaves
- 2 (15- or 16-oz.) cans black beans
- 4 or 5 ounces crumbled goat cheese

Heat the oil in a 3- or 4-quart saucepan over medium heat. Add the onion, bell pepper, garlic, and chile. Cook until onion is softened, about 5 minutes. Add the tomatoes, chili powder, paprika, salt, and oregano.

Process 1 can of the beans, with the liquid, in a blender or food processor until pureed. Drain remaining can of beans. Add the pureed beans and whole beans to the tomato mixture.

Cover; simmer 5 to 10 minutes. Serve in large individual soup bowls. Sprinkle each serving with goat cheese.

Gringo Chili

MAKES 5 OR 6 SERVINGS

Increase or decrease the amount of chili powder and jalapeño chile according to your family's taste.

1 (12-oz.) package hot pork sausage

1 yellow bell pepper, chopped

3 medium tomatoes, chopped

2 green onions, sliced

1 cup chicken broth or bouillon

1 clove garlic, crushed

2 teaspoons chili powder

1 jalapeño chile, seeded and finely chopped

½ teaspoon salt

1 (15- to 16-oz.) can refried beans

¼ cup sour cream or plain yogurt

1 cup crushed corn chips or tortilla chips

1 tablespoon chopped fresh cilantro

Cook the sausage in a 3-quart saucepan over medium heat until lightly browned, stirring to break up. Drain off fat.

Add the bell pepper, tomatoes, onions, broth, garlic, chili powder, chile, and salt. Simmer, covered, 25 to 30 minutes.

Stir in the refried beans; heat until bubbly, stirring frequently. Spoon into large individual bowls. Top with sour cream and corn chips. Sprinkle with the cilantro.

Pinto Turkey Chili

MAKES 6 TO 8 SERVINGS

CUT IT IN 1/2 FOR FOUR *FOUR*

Picante sauce plus chili powder provides a spicy flavor combination.

- 1 tablespoon vegetable oil
- 1 pound ground turkey
- 1 (28-oz.) can diced peeled tomatoes in tomato juice
- 1 cup bottled picante sauce
- 1 medium onion, chopped
- 2 medium zucchini, coarsely shredded
- 1 (15- to 16-oz.) can pinto beans, drained
- 1 tablespoon chili powder
- ¼ teaspoon ground cumin
- ½ teaspoon salt

Heat the oil in a 3-quart saucepan over medium heat. Add the turkey; cook until no longer pink, stirring to break up.

Add the tomatoes, picante sauce, onion, zucchini, pinto beans, chili powder, cumin, and salt. Simmer, covered, 40 to 45 minutes, or until onion is done.

Corn 'n' Bean Chili

MAKES 6 OR 7 SERVINGS

Give this chili a finishing touch with a dollop of your choice of yogurt or sour cream.

¾ pound lean boneless beef chuck, cut into ¾-inch cubes

1 tablespoon vegetable oil

1 medium onion, chopped

1 clove garlic, minced

1 red or green bell pepper, chopped

1 (27-oz.) can red kidney beans, drained

1 (8-oz.) can tomato sauce

1 teaspoon chili powder

½ teaspoon ground sage

¼ teaspoon ground cinnamon

1 (15- to 16-oz.) can whole-kernel corn, drained

1 (4-oz.) can chopped green chiles, drained

¼ cup plain yogurt or sour cream

2 tablespoons chopped cilantro

Brown the beef in the oil in a 4-quart Dutch oven or saucepan over medium-high heat, stirring occasionally. Add the onion, garlic, bell pepper, beans, tomato sauce, chili powder, sage, cinnamon, corn, and chiles.

Cover and cook over low heat about 1½ hours, or until beef is tender. Ladle into individual bowls. Top each with yogurt and chopped cilantro.

Fresh Tomato Chili

MAKES 4 SERVINGS.

Pepper Jack cheese has tiny pieces of spicy chile peppers swirled throughout.

1 pound lean ground beef

1 medium onion, chopped

1 clove garlic, minced

1 medium green or yellow bell pepper, chopped

3 medium tomatoes, peeled, seeded, and chopped

1 (8-oz.) can tomato sauce

2 teaspoons Worcestershire sauce

2 teaspoons chili powder

1 (14- to 15-oz.) can kidney beans, drained

¼ teaspoon salt

⅓ cup shredded pepper Jack cheese

Brown the ground beef in a 10-inch skillet over medium-high heat, stirring to break up. Add the onion, garlic, and bell pepper. Cook, stirring occasionally, 5 to 10 minutes. Drain off excess fat.

Add the tomatoes, tomato sauce, Worcestershire sauce, chili powder, kidney beans, and salt. Cover and simmer about 15 minutes. Spoon into bowls. Sprinkle with the cheese.

Green Chile Stew

MAKES 5 OR 6 SERVINGS

Choose one or all the toppings to highlight this hearty, spicy stew.

- **2 tablespoons vegetable oil**
- **1 pound boneless pork, cut into ½-inch cubes**
- **2 cups (½-inch cubes) potatoes**
- **1 large onion, chopped**
- **2 cloves garlic, crushed**
- **1 cup bottled green tomatillo salsa**
- **1 (14½-oz.) can diced tomatoes in tomato juice**
- **1 (7-oz.) can diced green chiles**
- **Sour cream, shredded Monterey Jack cheese, and chopped fresh cilantro leaves, for topping**

Heat the oil in a large saucepan over medium heat. Add the pork and cook until lightly browned.

Add the potatoes, onion, garlic, salsa, tomatoes, and chiles. Bring to a boil. Reduce heat; cover, and simmer 25 minutes, or until meat and potatoes are tender, stirring several times.

Serve in large bowls. Pass small bowls of sour cream, shredded cheese, and chopped cilantro for toppings.

Southwestern Cheese Soup

MAKES 5 OR 6 SERVINGS

Blue-corn tortilla chips are an ideal accompaniment to this rich, hearty soup.

2 tablespoons butter or margarine

1 small onion, chopped

1 cup chopped celery

3 large tomatoes, peeled, seeded, and chopped

2 small potatoes (about ½ pound), cut into ½-inch cubes

1 small clove garlic, crushed

1 teaspoon ground cumin

1 teaspoon finely chopped fresh oregano

½ teaspoon salt

3 tablespoons all-purpose flour

1 cup milk

2 cups half-and-half

¼ cup dry white wine

2 cups (8 ounces) shredded pepper Jack cheese

Melt the butter in a 2-quart saucepan over medium heat. Add the onion and celery. Cook until the onion is softened, about 5 minutes. Stir in the tomatoes, potatoes, garlic, cumin, oregano, and salt. Cook, stirring occasionally, until the potatoes are tender, about 15 minutes.

Whisk together the flour and milk. Remove the soup from heat. Add the flour mixture, stirring to mix. Return to heat. Stir in the half-and-half; cook, stirring constantly, until slightly thickened. Add the wine.

Remove from heat; gradually stir in the cheese until melted. Keep warm over low heat but do not allow to boil or soup will curdle.

Portuguese Red Bean Soup

MAKES 4 TO 6 SERVINGS

Make a complete meal with this hearty and flavorful soup.

8 ounces smoked sausage, cut into ¼-inch slices

1 (15½-oz.) can small red beans, undrained

1 (14½-oz.) can diced tomatoes with tomato juice

3 cups water

1 small onion, chopped

1 medium potato, diced

3 medium cloves garlic, thinly sliced crosswise

1 teaspoon sweet paprika

½ teaspoon salt or to taste

¼ teaspoon freshly ground black pepper

⅛ teaspoon ground cayenne pepper

2 cups lightly packed chopped green cabbage

¼ cup uncooked small elbow macaroni

1 tablespoon fresh lemon juice

Put the sausage into a large saucepan. Add the beans, tomatoes, water, onion, potato, garlic, paprika, salt, black pepper, and cayenne. Bring to a boil. Reduce heat, cover, and simmer 10 to 15 minutes, or until the potatoes are almost tender.

Stir in the cabbage, macaroni, and lemon juice. Cook, uncovered, 15 to 20 minutes, or until the potatoes and macaroni are tender, stirring occasionally.

Mediterranean Fish Stew

MAKES 5 OR 6 SERVINGS

Serve with crusty Italian or French bread and a tossed green salad.

2 tablespoons olive oil

1 small onion, finely chopped

4 large tomatoes, peeled, seeded, and chopped

1 (8-oz.) can tomato sauce

½ pound red potatoes, cut into ½-inch cubes

1 (8-oz.) bottle clam juice

¼ cup dry white wine

1 large clove garlic, minced

½ teaspoon fennel seeds, crushed

½ teaspoon dried leaf thyme, crushed

½ teaspoon dried leaf basil, crushed

1 large bay leaf

½ teaspoon salt

⅛ teaspoon freshly ground black pepper

1½ pounds boneless firm fish, cut into 1-inch chunks

⅓ cup chopped fresh parsley

Heat the oil in a 2-quart saucepan or Dutch oven over medium heat. Add the onion; sauté until softened, about 5 minutes.

Add the tomatoes, tomato sauce, potatoes, clam juice, wine, garlic, fennel seeds, thyme, basil, bay leaf, salt, and pepper. Bring to a boil. Reduce heat, cover, and simmer 15 to 20 minutes. Remove the bay leaf and discard.

Add the fish; simmer 12 to 15 minutes, or until fish turns from translucent to opaque. Stir in the parsley.

Turkey Stew & Rice

MAKES ABOUT 6 SERVINGS

An ideal dish to prepare when you have roast turkey left from a big family dinner.

3 carrots, cut into ½-inch slices

1 (16-oz.) package frozen Italian green beans

2 leeks, cut into ½-inch slices

1 tablespoon finely chopped parsley

3 cups chicken broth or turkey broth

1 teaspoon curry powder

½ teaspoon salt

⅛ teaspoon freshly ground black pepper

2 medium tomatoes, chopped

3 cups cubed cooked turkey

1 cup uncooked long-grain white rice

Combine the carrots, beans, leeks, parsley, broth, curry powder, salt, and pepper in a large saucepan. Cover and simmer about 15 minutes, or until the carrots are almost tender. Add the tomatoes and turkey. Cook another 5 minutes to allow flavors to blend.

Meanwhile, cook the rice according to package directions. Spoon rice into large individual soup bowls; cover with the turkey stew.

Border Town Bean Soup

MAKES ABOUT 4 SERVINGS

If you prefer tamer soup, you may substitute regular smoked sausage for the spicy sausage and a small mild green chile for the jalapeño.

> 1 cup dried pinto beans
>
> 2 (14½-oz.) cans beef broth
>
> 1 small onion, diced
>
> 3 tomatillos, husked and diced (see Note, page 59)
>
> 1 (11-oz.) can whole-kernel corn, drained
>
> ¼ pound spicy smoked link sausage, chopped
>
> 1 jalapeño chile, seeded and chopped
>
> 1 clove garlic, minced
>
> ½ teaspoon salt
>
> ¼ teaspoon freshly ground black pepper
>
> 1 tablespoon chopped fresh cilantro

Combine the beans and broth in a large saucepan. Bring to a boil. Reduce heat; simmer, covered, about 30 minutes. Add the onion, tomatillos, corn, sausage, chile, garlic, salt, and pepper.

Cover and simmer 1½ to 2 hours, or until the beans are done. Sprinkle with the cilantro.

Fennel, Leek, & Potato Soup

MAKES 4 OR 5 SERVINGS

A harmonious blend of good old-fashioned home cooking.

- 2 tablespoons butter or margarine
- 2 boneless, skinless chicken breast halves, cut into ½-inch pieces
- 2 fennel bulbs, thinly sliced
- 3 leeks, thinly sliced
- 4 medium potatoes, peeled and chopped
- ¼ teaspoon salt
- ¼ teaspoon freshly ground black pepper
- ¼ teaspoon seasoned salt
- 3 (14½-oz.) cans chicken broth

Melt the butter in a 4-quart saucepan over medium heat. Add the chicken; cook, stirring occasionally, until lightly browned, about 5 minutes.

Stir in the fennel, leeks, and potatoes. Add the salt, pepper, seasoned salt, and broth. Bring to a boil; reduce heat to medium-low. Cover and simmer about 20 minutes, or until vegetables are tender.

Meal-in-a-Bowl Minestrone

MAKES 4 TO 6 SERVINGS

Proscuitto, an Italian ham, adds a special flavor to this traditional vegetable soup.

    3 to 4 ounces proscuitto, chopped

    2 carrots, peeled and chopped

    2 stalks celery, chopped

    1 large onion, chopped

    2 medium potatoes, peeled and cut into 1-inch cubes

    1 (15-oz.) can diced Italian seasoned tomatoes

    1 (15-oz.) can garbanzo beans, drained

    ¼ cup chopped fresh Italian parsley

    1 teaspoon dried thyme leaves

    ¼ teaspoon freshly ground black pepper

    4 cups beef or chicken broth

    2 yellow zucchini or crookneck squash, chopped

    2 cups shredded napa cabbage

    2 cups fresh green beans, trimmed and cut into 1-inch pieces

    ⅓ cup freshly grated Parmesan cheese

Sauté the proscuitto, carrots, celery, and onion in a large saucepan over medium heat 10 minutes.

Stir in the potatoes, tomatoes, garbanzo beans, parsley, thyme, pepper, and broth. Cover and simmer over low heat 25 minutes.

Bring to a boil over medium-high heat. Stir in the zucchini, cabbage, and green beans. Cover and cook over medium-low heat 20 minutes, or until zucchini is tender. Ladle into bowls. Sprinkle with the Parmesan cheese.

Curried Carrot Soup

MAKES 4 OR 5 SERVINGS

Carrots and curry powder give this soup a beautiful orange color.

8 medium carrots, peeled and cut into 1-inch chunks

1 medium potato, peeled and cut into 1-inch chunks

1 small onion, coarsely chopped

1 teaspoon curry powder

½ teaspoon salt

⅛ teaspoon freshly ground black pepper

1 (14½-oz.) can chicken broth

1 (5-oz.) can evaporated milk

4 slices bacon, crisp-cooked

Combine the carrots, potato, onion, curry powder, salt, pepper, and broth in a 4-quart Dutch oven or saucepan over medium heat. Bring to a boil. Cover and cook over low heat 30 to 40 minutes, or until vegetables are tender.

Process the vegetables with a little of the hot broth in a food processor or blender until pureed; return to pot. Stir in the milk. Cover and heat until hot. Ladle into soup bowls. Crumble the bacon over each serving.

Fresh Corn Soup

MAKES 4 SERVINGS

Hominy enriches the fresh corn flavor. The Canadian bacon adds a rich smokiness.

1 tablespoon butter or margarine

1 medium onion, finely chopped

Kernels from 2 ears of corn (about 1 cup)

1 (14- to 15-oz.) can golden hominy, drained

2 medium tomatoes, chopped

1 (14½-oz.) can chicken broth

¼ teaspoon freshly ground black pepper

4 to 5 ounces Canadian bacon, coarsely chopped

2 tablespoons chopped fresh cilantro

Melt the butter in 4-quart Dutch oven or saucepan over medium heat. Add the onion and cook until softened, about 5 minutes.

Stir in the corn, hominy, tomatoes, broth, pepper, and bacon. Cover and cook over low heat about 30 minutes. Ladle into soup bowls. Sprinkle the cilantro over each serving.

Special Enough for Company

Sharing food around the table with friends and relatives can be a

rewarding and enriching experience. Get out the good china and

impress your guests with these special dishes. Enchiladas Verde

provide a surprising and delightful change from traditional

tomato-based enchiladas. Turkey Cannelloni with Cream Sauce

uses spring roll wrappers, instead of pasta tubes. Inside,

mortadella provides an added surprise to the savory filling.

Creamy Basil Pasta

Enchiladas Verde

Greek Pastitsio

Hoisin-Glazed Pizza

Italian-Style Flank Steak

Mango-Mustard Chicken

Occidental Chicken

South Seas Chicken Pizza

Tortilla Sausage Strata

Tarragon Fish Kabobs with Lemon Rice

Turkey Cannelloni with Cream Sauce

Chicken with Watermelon–Jicama Salsa

Baked Chicken with Fruited Salsa

Turkey Vindaloo

Layered Lamb, Okra, & Couscous Bake

Curried Pork & Rice

Milanese Special

Creamy Basil Pasta

MAKES 4 SERVINGS

A memorable fresh basil flavor makes this an elegant-tasting creation.

⅓ cup sun-dried tomatoes (dry pack)

8 ounces uncooked gnocchi or orchette pasta

2 tablespoons butter or margarine

2 zucchini, chopped

1 cup small crimini mushrooms, quartered

1 (6-oz.) jar artichoke hearts in water, drained and sliced

1 cup cubed cooked chicken

3 tablespoons all-purpose flour

1 (14½-oz.) can chicken broth

1 cup fresh basil leaves

1 cup half-and-half

1 cup freshly grated Parmesan cheese

Cover the sun-dried tomatoes with boiling water; let soak 15 minutes to soften. Drain, chop, and set aside.

Cook the pasta according to package directions. Drain and toss with 1 tablespoon of the butter.

Melt the remaining 1 tablespoon of butter in a large skillet over medium heat. Stir in the zucchini. Cook, stirring, until almost tender. Add the mushrooms, artichokes, chicken, and reserved tomatoes. Sprinkle with the flour; stir to combine. Gradually stir in the broth. Cook, stirring, until thickened and bubbly.

In a blender or food processor, puree the basil and half-and-half until very finely chopped. Add to skillet along with the pasta and cheese. Heat, stirring occasionally, until hot.

Enchiladas Verde

MAKES 4 SERVINGS

A universally loved Mexican favorite made mild but with plenty of flavor.

½ **pound ground turkey**

1 **(16-oz.) jar salsa verde**

1 **(10-oz.) package frozen chopped spinach, thawed and squeezed dry**

¼ **cup butter or margarine**

⅓ **cup all-purpose flour**

3 **cups chicken broth**

1 **cup loosely packed cilantro leaves**

2 **tablespoons vegetable oil**

8 **(6-inch) corn tortillas**

1 **(3-oz.) package cream cheese, cut into 8 strips**

1 **cup (4 ounces) shredded Monterey Jack cheese**

Cook the turkey in a large nonstick skillet over medium heat until no longer pink, stirring to break up. Reserve 1½ cups of salsa; set aside. Stir the remaining ½ cup salsa and spinach into turkey. Set aside to cool slightly.

Melt the butter in a medium saucepan over medium-high heat; stir in flour until smooth. Gradually stir in the broth. Cook, stirring, until thickened and bubbly. Remove from heat.

Preheat oven to 350F (175C). Grease a 13 x 9-inch baking dish. In a blender or food processor, combine the remaining salsa and cilantro; process until very finely chopped. Stir into thickened broth; set aside.

Heat the oil in a small skillet over medium-low heat. Add tortillas, one at a time. Heat each side about 5 seconds to soften, then drain briefly on paper towels. While the tortillas are still warm, place about ⅓ cup of the turkey mixture along center of each tortilla. Top with 1 strip of cream cheese. Roll up and place, seam side down, in the prepared dish. Pour the reserved sauce over the filled tortillas. Sprinkle with the Monterey Jack cheese.

Bake 25 minutes, or until bubbly. Serve 2 tortillas per person.

Greek Pastitsio

A flavorful Greek meat and pasta dish, it is enrobed in a rich custard.

1 pound lean ground beef or lamb

1 onion, chopped

2 cloves garlic, minced

1 (8-oz.) can tomato sauce

1 teaspoon ground allspice

½ teaspoon salt

8 ounces uncooked ziti or tortiglioni

8 tablespoons (1 stick) butter or margarine

1 (10-oz.) package frozen spinach, thawed and drained

⅓ cup all-purpose flour

3¾ cups milk

½ teaspoon ground nutmeg

4 eggs

1 cup freshly grated Parmesan cheese

Cook the beef, onion, and garlic in a large skillet over medium-high heat until the beef is no longer pink, stirring to break up. Drain off excess fat. Stir in the tomato sauce, allspice, and salt. Simmer, uncovered, over low heat about 20 minutes or until thickened.

Preheat oven to 325F (165C). Grease a 13 × 9-inch baking dish. Cook the pasta according to package directions; drain. Toss with 2 tablespoons of the butter. Place half of the pasta in the prepared dish. Top with the beef mixture then the spinach. Spread the remaining pasta over the spinach.

Melt the remaining 6 tablespoons butter in a medium saucepan over medium heat. Stir in the flour and cook until bubbly. Gradually stir in the milk. Cook, stirring, until thickened and bubbly. Stir in the nutmeg; remove from heat.

Beat the eggs in a small bowl. Stir in about ½ cup of the hot milk mixture into eggs. Stir the egg mixture back into the milk mixture. Stir in ½ cup of the cheese. Pour cheese mixture over the pasta. Sprinkle with the remaining cheese.

Bake about 25 minutes, or until topping is lightly browned. Let stand 10 minutes before serving.

Hoisin-Glazed Pizza

MAKES ABOUT 4 SERVINGS

Wonderful Asian spices and smoked pork combine to make a tasty pizza.

2 tablespoons soy sauce

2 tablespoons white wine

3 tablespoons hoisin sauce

2 tablespoons ketchup

2 tablespoons honey

1 tablespoon grated fresh ginger

1 clove garlic, minced

¼ teaspoon five-spice powder or allspice

2 carrots, coarsely shredded

4 boneless smoked cooked pork chops, cut into 2-inch strips

3 green onions, cut into 1-inch slices

1 tablespoon cornstarch

½ cup chicken broth

1 (12-inch) prebaked thin pizza crust

2 tablespoons chopped fresh cilantro

Preheat oven to 450F (230C). Combine the soy sauce, wine, hoisin sauce, ketchup, honey, ginger, garlic, five-spice powder, carrots, and pork in a medium saucepan. Cook, stirring occasionally, over medium heat about 10 minutes. Add the onions.

Dissolve the cornstarch in the broth. Stir into the pork mixture; bring to a boil. Reduce heat and cook, stirring occasionally, 2 minutes.

Place the crust on a baking sheet; spread the filling over the crust.

Bake about 8 minutes, or until hot. Sprinkle with cilantro; cut into wedges.

Italian-Style Flank Steak

MAKES 6 TO 8 SERVINGS

When sliced crosswise, this stuffed steak forms attractive spiral slices.

1 (10-oz.) package frozen spinach

1 small red bell pepper, chopped

½ cup Italian-flavored dry bread crumbs

1 clove garlic, minced

¼ cup pine nuts, toasted (see Tip, page 25)

1 egg, slightly beaten

1 (1½- to-2 pound) beef flank steak

¼ cup freshly grated Parmesan cheese

6 to 8 medium baking potatoes, peeled

1 tablespoon butter or margarine, melted

Preheat oven to 350F (175C). Thaw the spinach in a large strainer; press with back of spoon to remove excess liquid. Combine the spinach, bell pepper, bread crumbs, garlic, pine nuts, and egg in a medium bowl.

Pound the steak between sheets of plastic wrap to ½-inch thickness. Spread the spinach mixture on one side of steak. Sprinkle with Parmesan cheese. Roll up steak, jelly-roll style, from one long side. Tie with kitchen twine at 3-inch intervals.

Brush the potatoes with the butter. Place steak and potatoes in a roasting pan. Cover and roast about 30 minutes. Uncover and cook 30 to 45 minutes, or until potatoes are tender. Cut steak crosswise into 1-inch-thick slices.

Mango-Mustard Chicken

MAKES 4 TO 6 SERVINGS

Chicken dressed up with sesame seeds and a tropical mango sauce only needs a green salad and an easy dessert such as brownies with ice cream to make a company meal.

1 fresh mango, peeled and chopped

1 tablespoon Dijon mustard

1 clove garlic, minced

¼ teaspoon curry powder

¼ teaspoon salt

⅛ teaspoon freshly ground black pepper

1 (3 ½- to 4-pound) frying chicken, cut into pieces

3 tablespoons vegetable oil

2 tablespoons sesame seeds

4 sweet potatoes, peeled and quartered

Stir the mango, mustard, garlic, curry powder, salt, and pepper in a small bowl; set aside.

Brush the chicken with 2 tablespoons of the oil; coat with the sesame seeds. Brown the chicken on all sides in a 12-inch skillet over medium-high heat.

Brush the potatoes with the remaining 1 tablespoon oil; arrange around chicken. Cover and cook over medium-low heat until potatoes and chicken are tender, about 45 minutes. Spoon mango sauce over chicken and potatoes.

Occidental Chicken

MAKES 6 SERVINGS

Coconut milk gives this dish a somewhat sweet exotic taste.

- 2 tablespoons all-purpose flour
- 1 tablespoon curry powder
- 1 teaspoon ground cumin
- ½ teaspoon salt
- ⅛ teaspoon cayenne pepper
- 6 chicken breasts or thighs
- 2 tablespoons vegetable oil
- 1 clove garlic, minced
- 1 jalapeño chile, seeded and minced
- 1 cup coconut milk (see Note, below)
- 4 brown mushrooms, chopped
- 2 green onions, chopped
- 1 cup uncooked long-grain white rice

Combine the flour, curry powder, cumin, salt, and cayenne in a plastic bag. Add the chicken and shake to coat. Refrigerate at least 1 hour.

Heat the oil in large skillet over medium-high heat. Add the chicken and cook until browned, turning. Stir in garlic, chile, coconut milk, mushrooms, and onions. Cover and simmer 30 minutes. Simmer, uncovered, until chicken is tender, 10 to 15 minutes.

Cook the rice according to package directions. Serve the chicken over the rice.

NOTE

Coconut milk is available in cans, but do not confuse it with cream of coconut, which is used to make drinks. Coconut milk is made by processing the shredded coconut meat with water.

South Seas Chicken Pizza

MAKES 4 TO 6 SERVINGS

A unique way to use cooked chicken or turkey.

1 (12-inch) prebaked thin pizza crust

1 tablespoon minced fresh chives

1 tablespoon minced fresh cilantro

1 small jalapeño chile, seeded and minced

1 (8-oz.) package cream cheese, softened

1 cup finely chopped cooked chicken

1 papaya, peeled, seeded, and sliced

1 kiwifruit, peeled and sliced

½ cup fresh or canned diced pineapple

¼ cup coconut, toasted (see Tip, below)

Preheat oven to 425F (220C). Place crust on a baking sheet. Bake about 5 minutes, or until hot.

Stir together the chives, cilantro, chile, and cream cheese in a small bowl.

Spread the cream cheese mixture over the warm crust. Arrange the chicken and fruit over the cream cheese, pressing lightly into cheese spread. Sprinkle with the toasted coconut. Cut into wedges. Serve immediately.

TIP

To toast coconut: Preheat oven to 350F (175C). Spread coconut in a 9-inch pie pan. Toast 6 to 8 minutes, or until golden; set aside to cool.

Tortilla Sausage Strata

MAKES 4 OR 5 SERVINGS

This layered treat makes a wonderful brunch or supper.

¾ pound bulk pork sausage

1 small red or green bell pepper, chopped

4 green onions, thinly sliced

9 (6-inch) corn tortillas

1 cup green chile picante sauce

3 eggs, slightly beaten

1½ cups milk

½ cup (2 ounces) pepper Jack cheese

Preheat oven to 325F (165C). Grease a 9-inch-square baking dish. Crumble the sausage into a hot 10-inch skillet over medium heat. Add the bell pepper. Cook, stirring to break up sausage, until sausage is brown. Stir in the onions.

Arrange 3 of the tortillas in the bottom of prepared dish. Top with one third each of the sausage mixture and picante sauce. Repeat with another third of the tortillas, sausage mixture, and picante sauce. Repeat layers, ending with picante sauce. Combine the eggs and milk in a medium bowl. Pour over all. Sprinkle with cheese.

Bake 40 to 50 minutes, or until filling is set. Cut into pieces and serve warm.

Tarragon Fish Kabobs with Lemon Rice

MAKES 4 TO 6 SERVINGS

The Mediterranean flavors of the kabobs blend well with the lemony rice.

⅓ cup olive oil

4 tablespoons fresh lemon juice

1 tablespoon minced fresh tarragon

2 cloves garlic, minced

½ teaspoon sugar

½ teaspoon salt

¼ teaspoon freshly ground black pepper

1 pound (1-inch-thick) fish fillets, cut into 1-inch cubes

2 Japanese eggplants

1 (14½-oz.) can chicken broth

1 tablespoon butter

1 cup uncooked white basmati rice

12 to 16 small mushrooms

1 onion, cut into chunks

2 tablespoons chopped fresh parsley

In a shallow glass dish, combine the oil, 2 tablespoons of the lemon juice, the tarragon, garlic, sugar, salt, and pepper. Add the fish and stir to coat. Cover and refrigerate several hours or overnight. Remove the fish; reserve the marinade.

Steam the eggplant 3 to 4 minutes; let cool slightly. Cut the eggplant into ¾- to 1-inch-diagonal slices and coat with reserved marinade. Set aside.

Bring the broth, remaining 2 tablespoons of the lemon juice, and the butter to a boil in a medium saucepan over high heat. Stir in the rice; cover. Reduce heat to low and cook 17 minutes. Stir; re-cover and remove from heat. Let stand 5 minutes.

Preheat broiler or grill. Thread the eggplant, fish, mushrooms, and onion on 4 to 6 (12-inch) skewers. Brush with any remaining marinade. Broil or grill 4 to 5 inches from heat 5 to 6 minutes. Turn and broil 3 to 4 minutes or until fish flakes. Spoon rice into a large platter; top with kabobs. Garnish with parsley.

Turkey Cannelloni with Cream Sauce

MAKES 6 SERVINGS; 12 CANNELLONI

This is an unusual and mouthwatering addition to any buffet table.

1 tablespoon vegetable oil

1¼ pounds lean ground turkey

⅓ pound mortadella, coarsely chopped (about 1 cup)

1 (10-oz.) package frozen chopped spinach, thawed and squeezed dry

4 green onions, chopped

2 tablespoons chopped fresh Italian parsley

1 cup chopped fresh mushrooms

1 tablespoon chopped fresh oregano

½ teaspoon salt

¼ teaspoon freshly ground black pepper

⅓ cup fine dry bread crumbs

2 eggs, slightly beaten

4 ounces fontina cheese, shredded (1 cup)

12 (about 6-inch-square) spring roll or egg roll wrappers

¼ cup butter or margarine

¼ cup all-purpose flour

1 cup chicken broth

1 cup half-and-half

⅛ teaspoon ground nutmeg

Preheat oven to 375F (190C). Heat the oil in large nonstick skillet over medium heat; add the turkey. Cook, stirring to break up, until no longer pink. Add the mortadella, spinach, onions, parsley, mushrooms, oregano, salt, and pepper. Cook 1 minute. Remove from heat; stir in the bread crumbs, eggs, and cheese.

Spoon one twelfth of the turkey mixture diagonally along the center of an egg roll wrapper. Fold the bottom corner over the filling, then fold in the 2 corners. Starting at the bottom, roll up. Place, seam side down, in a 13 × 9-inch baking dish. Repeat with remaining turkey mixture and wrappers.

Melt the butter in a small saucepan over medium heat. Stir in the flour and cook until bubbly. Stir in the broth, half-and-half, and nutmeg. Cook, stirring, until thickened. Pour over cannelloni in pan.

Bake 20 to 25 minutes, or until top is lightly browned.

Chicken with Watermelon–Jicama Salsa

MAKES 6 SERVINGS

Jicama is a large brown turnip-shaped root vegetable with a crispy white interior. It is available in most produce sections.

2 tablespoons vegetable oil

1 teaspoon ground ginger

¼ teaspoon salt

⅛ teaspoon freshly ground black pepper

1 clove garlic, minced

6 boneless, skinless chicken breast halves

2 medium zucchini, sliced

1 (10-oz.) package dry plain couscous (see Note, below)

WATERMELON-JICAMA SALSA

1 cup coarsely shredded jicama

1 cup small watermelon cubes

¼ cup finely chopped red onion

¼ cup chopped fresh cilantro

1 tablespoon fresh lime juice

Combine the oil, ginger, salt, pepper, and garlic in a small bowl. Brush seasoned oil on the chicken. Heat a 10- to 12-inch skillet over medium-high heat. Add the chicken and cook until brown, about 5 minutes. Turn the chicken. Add the zucchini. Cover and cook over medium-low heat until chicken and zucchini are tender, about 10 minutes.

Prepare the salsa: In a medium bowl, combine all the ingredients; set aside.

Cook the couscous according to package directions. Spoon into a platter; top with chicken mixture. Serve with salsa.

NOTE

Packaged couscous is precooked medium-grained semolina (coarsely ground durum wheat). Because it is precooked, it doesn't need further cooking. Just add to boiling water and allow to stand, covered, about 5 minutes or until plump and tender.

Baked Chicken with Fruited Salsa

MAKES 5 OR 6 SERVINGS

An easy-to-assemble casserole, it is accented by a fruity salsa.

FRUITED SALSA

1 mango, peeled and cubed

1 (11-oz.) can Mexi-corn, drained

1 cup fresh or canned pineapple chunks, drained

CHICKEN

1 ¼ cups uncooked long-grain white rice

1 (14 ½ oz.) can chicken broth

1 (12-oz.) jar or 1 ½ cups thick prepared tomato salsa

¼ teaspoon salt

⅛ teaspoon freshly ground black pepper

5 or 6 boneless, skinless chicken breast halves

Preheat oven to 350F (175C). Grease a 2 ½ quart casserole dish. Prepare the salsa: Combine all the salsa ingredients in a medium bowl. Cover and refrigerate.

Stir together the rice, broth, tomato salsa, salt, and pepper in prepared dish. Place the chicken on top of the rice mixture. Cover tightly. Bake 1 ½ hours, or until chicken and rice are tender. Serve with the Fruited Salsa.

Turkey Vindaloo

MAKES ABOUT 6 SERVINGS

Vindaloo is a type of Indian curry seasoned with vinegar.

¼ cup white wine vinegar

3 cloves garlic, minced

1 tablespoon grated fresh ginger

2 teaspoons ground cumin

½ teaspoon ground allspice

¼ teaspoon ground cloves

¼ teaspoon crushed red pepper flakes

½ teaspoon salt

3 tablespoons olive or vegetable oil

2 boneless, skinless turkey thighs, cut into 1- to 2-inch pieces

1 large onion, chopped

1 (14- to 16-oz.) can diced tomatoes with juice

1 cup uncooked white basmati rice

⅓ cup chopped fresh cilantro

In a blender or food processor, combine the vinegar, garlic, ginger, cumin, allspice, cloves, pepper flakes, salt, and 1 tablespoon of the oil. Blend until smooth. Place the turkey in a large bowl; pour the vinegar mixture over. Toss to coat; cover. Refrigerate several hours or overnight.

Heat the remaining 2 tablespoons of oil in a 3- to 4-quart saucepan over medium heat. Add the onion and cook, stirring occasionally, 5 minutes.

Stir in the tomatoes, turkey, and marinade. Simmer, covered, over low heat about 40 minutes. Uncover; simmer 15 to 20 minutes.

Meanwhile, cook the rice according to package directions. Spoon the rice into a platter. Stir the cilantro into the turkey mixture and spoon over the rice.

Layered Lamb, Okra, & Couscous Bake

MAKES 4 OR 5 SERVINGS

Serve this Mediterranean casserole as part of an adventuresome menu. Add a fresh fruit salad, perhaps made with some fruits that you have not tried before, and warm pita bread.

1 pound fresh or frozen whole okra

1 tablespoon vegetable oil

1 pound lean ground lamb

1 onion, chopped

4 tomatoes, peeled, seeded, and chopped

2 cloves garlic, minced

½ teaspoon salt

¼ teaspoon freshly ground black pepper

1 (10¾ oz.) can condensed beef broth

⅓ cup plain yogurt

1 cup dry couscous (see Note, page 165)

Preheat oven to 350F (175C). Grease a 2½- to 3-quart baking dish. Trim the stems from the okra. Heat about 1 inch of water in a large skillet. Add okra; bring to a boil. Reduce heat to medium-low. Cover and cook 5 minutes. Drain okra and set aside.

Heat the oil in a large skillet over medium-high heat. Add the lamb and onion. Cook, stirring to break up lamb, 2 to 3 minutes. Stir in the tomatoes, garlic, salt, pepper, and broth. Simmer, covered, 15 minutes. Remove from heat. Stir in the yogurt.

Place one third of the lamb mixture in bottom of the prepared dish. Sprinkle half of the couscous on the lamb mixture. Arrange half of the okra on the couscous. Repeat layers with remaining ingredients ending with the lamb mixture.

Cover and bake 35 to 45 minutes, or until liquid is absorbed and couscous is tender.

Curried Pork & Rice

MAKES 5 OR 6 SERVINGS

A sprinkle of chopped peanuts and a bit of chutney provide the finishing touches to this easy skillet dish.

 1 tablespoon vegetable oil

 5 or 6 boneless pork chops or cutlets

 1 cup uncooked long-grain white rice

 2 medium tomatoes, peeled and diced

 1 small onion, chopped

 1 clove garlic, crushed

 2 cups chicken broth

 1 teaspoon curry powder

 ½ teaspoon salt

 ⅛ teaspoon freshly ground black pepper

Heat the oil in a 10-inch skillet over medium heat. Add the pork chops; cook until lightly browned on both sides, about 10 minutes.

Add the rice, tomatoes, onion, garlic, broth, curry powder, salt, and pepper. Cover and simmer 35 to 45 minutes, or until the chops and rice are tender and most of the liquid has been absorbed.

VARIATION
Chicken pieces can be substituted for the pork. Simmer about 30 minutes.

Milanese Special

MAKES 4 TO 6 SERVINGS

Several classic Italian ingredients are used to create a delicious pasta dish.

1 fennel bulb, very thinly sliced

1 large onion, thinly sliced

4 ounces pancetta, coarsely chopped

1 (28-oz.) can diced tomatoes

¼ teaspoon salt

⅛ teaspoon freshly ground black pepper

8 ounces uncooked linguine or fettuccini

Freshly grated Parmesan cheese or Romano cheese

Combine the fennel, onion, pancetta, tomatoes, salt, and pepper in a large skillet. Cover and simmer 30 to 35 minutes, or until fennel is softened.

Meanwhile, cook the pasta according to package directions; drain. Rinse and drain again. Add the pasta to the skillet. Sprinkle with cheese to taste; toss to combine.

Brunches & Light Meals

Are you too busy during the week to have a leisurely meal with

family and friends? Enjoy an easy weekend brunch featuring one of

the dishes in this chapter. I have also included some pizzas for you

to enjoy; the Zucchini Sausage Pizza has a surprise—the crust is

made of zucchini, not pizza dough. If you're hungry for a light

meal or snack, try one of the delicious sandwiches such as the

Beefy Roquefort Sandwiches or the Smoked Chicken Focaccia. The

taste of French Cabbage Croissants will take you to a Paris bistro;

enjoy the journey.

Beefy Roquefort Sandwiches

BLT Dinner Stack

French Cabbage Croissants

Smoked Chicken Focaccia

Sesame Halibut Sandwiches

Zucchini Triangles

Grandma's Favorite Brunch

Baked Tomato & Cheese Sandwiches

Tomato Cheese Muffins

Spinach & Egg Brunch Muffins

Brunch Pasta Pie

Skillet Sunday Brunch

Sausage-Macaroni Quiche

Pizza Brunch Special

Chili Pizza

Zucchini Sausage Pizza

Beefy Roquefort Sandwiches

MAKES 6 OPEN-FACED SANDWICHES

Tangy, thick Roquefort salad dressing provides richness to these satisfying sandwiches.

²⁄₃ **cup refrigerated thick Roquefort dressing**

1 ½ **cups (6 ounces) shredded Monterey Jack cheese**

2 **teaspoons prepared horseradish**

2 **tablespoons finely chopped fresh parsley**

3 **(7- to 8-inch) French rolls, split in half lengthwise**

12 **ounces thinly sliced roast beef**

1 **large tomato, thinly sliced**

6 **thin red onion slices**

Preheat broiler. Combine the dressing, cheese, horseradish, and parsley in a small bowl. Spread half of the dressing mixture on cut sides of each roll. Place rolls, cut sides up, on a baking sheet.

Broil the sandwiches 4 to 5 inches from heat 1 to 2 minutes, or until bubbly. Arrange the beef, tomato, and onion on rolls. Spoon the remaining cheese mixture over each sandwich. Place under broiler and heat until bubbly. Serve immediately.

BLT Dinner Stack

MAKES 4 SERVINGS

This is the time-honored bacon, lettuce, and tomato sandwich with a new twist.

> 4 large slices sheepherder bread, toasted
>
> ¼ cup mayonnaise
>
> 5 cups shredded iceberg lettuce
>
> 12 strips thick sliced bacon, cooked until crisp
>
> 1 large tomato, sliced
>
> 1½ cups (6 ounces) shredded sharp Cheddar cheese

Preheat broiler. Place the toast on a large baking sheet. Spread top of each slice with mayonnaise. Arrange lettuce on each slice. Arrange bacon and then tomato over the lettuce. Sprinkle the cheese over each sandwich.

Broil the sandwiches 4 to 5 inches from heat 1 to 2 minutes, or until cheese melts. Place each sandwich on an individual plate. Serve immediately.

French Cabbage Croissants

MAKES 6 SERVINGS

These sandwiches, reminiscent of a French bistro cabbage pie, make a flavorful supper.

½ pound bacon, coarsely chopped

¾ pound bulk pork sausage

2 onions, coarsely chopped

1 small head cabbage, shredded

½ teaspoon salt

¼ teaspoon freshly ground black pepper

1 cup chopped mushrooms

6 large croissants

Cook the bacon in a large skillet over medium heat until it begins to brown. Stir in the sausage and cook, stirring to break up, until it is no longer pink.

Add the onions, cabbage, salt, and pepper. Cook, covered, over medium-low heat about 30 minutes. Stir in the mushrooms; cook 5 minutes. Drain off all liquid.

Preheat oven to 400F (205C). Split the croissants in half horizontally. Place one sixth of the filling on each croissant bottom. Replace tops. Place on a baking sheet; bake 5 to 10 minutes, or until warmed.

Smoked Chicken Focaccia

MAKES 6 SERVINGS

A sun-dried tomato or onion-herb focaccia goes particularly well with this filling.

2 cups finely chopped smoked chicken or turkey

2 tablespoons minced green onion

1 stalk celery, finely chopped

1 (4- to 5-oz.) carton garlic and herb cheese spread

¼ cup slivered almonds, toasted (see Tip, page 25)

1 (14-oz.) loaf focaccia

Preheat oven to 350F (175C). Combine the chicken, onion, celery, cheese spread, and almonds in a medium bowl.

Split the bread in half lengthwise. Place the bottom half on a baking sheet; spread the chicken mixture over the cut side. Replace the top. Cut the filled loaf into 6 equal pieces. Cover with foil and bake 20 minutes. Uncover and bake 5 minutes, or until heated through. Serve immediately.

Sesame Halibut Sandwiches

MAKES 4 SERVINGS

Try this fish sandwich for a change from grilled hamburgers.

¼ cup toasted sesame seeds

2 green onions, minced

1 clove garlic, minced

1 tablespoon soy sauce

2 teaspoons fresh lime juice

1 teaspoon sesame oil

1 teaspoon honey

4 Kaiser rolls

4 (about 1-inch-thick) halibut or swordfish fillets

1 tablespoon vegetable oil

1 cup sprouts

Preheat broiler or grill. Oil a broiler pan or grill. Combine the sesame seeds, onions, garlic, soy sauce, lime juice, sesame oil, and honey in a small bowl. Spread on the rolls; set aside.

Brush the fish with vegetable oil. Place on prepared pan or grill. Broil or grill 4 to 5 inches from heat 3 to 5 minutes on each side, or until fish flakes easily. Place on bottom half of rolls; add sprouts. Replace tops of rolls. Serve hot.

Zucchini Triangles

MAKES 6 SERVINGS

These attractive turnovers are similar to Italian calzones. Using refrigerated pizza dough makes them easy to do.

½ pound bulk sweet Italian sausage

1 small onion, chopped

½ teaspoon salt

⅛ teaspoon crushed red pepper flakes

1 clove garlic, minced

½ teaspoon dried oregano

2 medium zucchini, coarsely chopped

1 cup (4 ounces) shredded cheddarella cheese

1 (10-oz.) package refrigerated pizza crust dough

Preheat oven to 400F (205C). Grease a large baking sheet. Heat a skillet over medium heat. Stir in the sausage, onion, salt, pepper flakes, garlic, oregano, and zucchini. Cook until sausage is brown, 5 to 10 minutes, stirring to break up. Drain well; stir in ½ cup of the cheese.

Roll the dough out to a 15 × 10-inch rectangle; cut into 6 (5-inch) squares. Spoon one sixth of the filling in center of each square of dough. Fold opposite corners together to form a triangle. Pinch or crimp edges to seal. Sprinkle each triangle with the remaining cheese.

Bake 15 to 18 minutes, or until golden brown. Serve hot.

Grandma's Favorite Brunch

MAKES 4 SERVINGS

For a very hearty brunch, serve with scrambled eggs and toast.

1 (12-oz.) package bulk pork sausage

1 (15-oz.) can hominy, drained

1 small onion, thinly sliced

1 mild green chile, seeded and chopped

3 tomatoes, peeled, seeded, and chopped

½ cup (2 ounces) shredded Cheddar cheese (optional)

Sauté the sausage until brown in a large skillet over medium heat, stirring to break up; discard excess fat.

Add the hominy, onion, and chile. Cook, stirring occasionally, 5 to 10 minutes. Stir in the tomatoes and cook 2 or 3 minutes to combine flavors. Sprinkle with the cheese, if desired. Serve hot.

Baked Tomato & Cheese Sandwiches

MAKES 4 SANDWICHES

Great for brunch, lunch, or a midnight snack, this warm sandwich is somewhat reminiscent of Welsh rarebit but with tomatoes and bacon.

3 tablespoons butter or margarine

3 tablespoons all-purpose flour

½ teaspoon dry mustard

¼ teaspoon salt

⅛ teaspoon ground white pepper

1 cup milk

4 (½-inch-thick) slices rye bread or French bread, toasted

8 (¼-inch-thick) tomato slices

4 bacon slices, crisp-cooked and crumbled

1 cup (4 ounces) shredded Swiss cheese

Sweet paprika

Preheat oven to 350F (175C). Melt the butter in a medium saucepan over low heat; blend in the flour, dry mustard, salt, and white pepper. Cook, stirring, until smooth and bubbly. Stir in the milk. Cook over medium heat, stirring constantly, until thickened. Set aside.

Place the toast on a baking sheet. Top each slice of toast with 2 tomato slices, then one fourth of the crumbled bacon and ¼ cup sauce. Top each with ¼ cup of the cheese and a dash of paprika.

Bake 20 minutes, or until heated. Serve hot.

VARIATION
Substitute shredded Cheddar cheese for the Swiss cheese.

Tomato Cheese Muffins

MAKES 12 MUFFINS

Serve these new-flavored, old-fashioned muffins with a large salad for a light lunch. They are also a wonderful accompaniment to grilled pork or beef.

2 ½ cups all-purpose flour

1 ½ teaspoons baking powder

½ teaspoon baking soda

1 teaspoon instant minced onion

½ teaspoon salt

2 tablespoons sugar

1 tablespoon chopped fresh basil or 1 teaspoon dried

2 eggs, slightly beaten

1 medium tomato, peeled, seeded, and chopped

½ cup milk

2 tablespoons ketchup

¼ cup butter or margarine, melted and cooled

¾ cup (3 ounces) shredded Cheddar cheese

Preheat oven to 375F (190C). Line 12 standard muffin cups with fluted paper liners or grease 12 muffin cups; set aside. Combine the flour, baking powder, baking soda, instant onion, salt, sugar, and basil in a medium bowl. Combine the eggs, tomato, milk, ketchup, and butter in another bowl.

Add the tomato mixture and ½ cup of the cheese to the dry ingredients; stir until just moistened. Spoon equal amounts into prepared muffin cups. Sprinkle tops with the remaining ¼ cup cheese.

Bake about 18 minutes, or until golden brown. Serve warm.

Spinach & Egg Brunch Muffins

MAKES 6 SERVINGS

These are perfect knife-and-fork open-faced sandwiches for a weekend brunch or a special weekday breakfast when you're tired of your traditional fare.

1 (9½- to 10-oz.) package frozen creamed spinach

3 hard-cooked eggs, peeled and chopped

4 bacon slices, crisp-cooked

1 green onion, finely chopped

1 teaspoon Worcestershire sauce

6 English muffin halves, toasted

2 medium tomatoes, chopped

¾ cup (3 ounces) shredded mozzarella cheese

Preheat broiler. Cook the spinach according to package directions. Combine the cooked spinach, eggs, bacon, onion, and Worcestershire sauce in a small bowl. Spoon about ¼ cup of the spinach mixture on each toasted muffin half. Top each with equal amounts of chopped tomatoes and then cheese. Place the muffin halves on a baking sheet. Broil until cheese melts.

VARIATION

If creamed spinach is not available, cook 1 (10-oz.) package frozen chopped spinach according to package directions. Drain well and stir spinach, eggs, bacon, onion, and Worcestershire sauce into 2 cups medium white sauce made using 4 table-spoons flour, 4 tablespoons butter, and 2 cups milk.

Brunch Pasta Pie

MAKES 6 SERVINGS

The pasta forms the shell for the custardy filling. Serve for brunch or lunch with crusty bread and a green salad.

4 ounces uncooked vermicelli

2 tablespoons vegetable oil

3 medium tomatoes, sliced

3 eggs, slightly beaten

1 cup milk

1 tablespoon Dijon mustard

½ teaspoon prepared horseradish

¼ teaspoon salt

⅛ teaspoon freshly ground black pepper

¼ cup finely chopped green or yellow bell pepper

⅓ cup thin slivers of pepperoni or salami (1½ to 2 ounces)

1 teaspoon finely chopped fresh parsley

Preheat oven to 350F (175C). Cook the pasta according to package directions; drain.

Add the oil to the pasta; toss the pasta until well coated. Press the pasta into the bottom and sides of a 10-inch shallow baking dish. Top with the tomato slices. Combine the eggs, milk, mustard, horseradish, salt, and pepper in a medium bowl. Pour over the tomatoes. Top with the bell pepper and pepperoni. Sprinkle with the parsley.

Bake 35 to 40 minutes, or until firm. Serve warm.

Skillet Sunday Brunch

MAKES 4 OR 5 SERVINGS

Assemble everyone before you put the eggs on, because this dish is at its very best as soon as it is done.

1 tablespoon olive or vegetable oil

3 ounces prosciutto, cut into small strips (about ½ cup)

1 small onion, chopped

5 large tomatoes, peeled, seeded, and chopped

3 or 4 large mushrooms, diced

1 tablespoon chopped fresh basil

¼ teaspoon salt

⅛ teaspoon freshly ground black pepper

1 teaspoon Worcestershire sauce

4 or 5 eggs

2 tablespoons freshly grated Parmesan cheese

4 or 5 English muffin halves

Heat the oil in a large skillet over low heat. Add the prosciutto and onion; cook until onion is softened, about 10 minutes. Stir in the tomatoes, mushrooms, basil, salt, pepper, and Worcestershire sauce. Cook, uncovered, over medium heat until slightly thickened, about 15 minutes, stirring occasionally.

With the back of a wooden spoon, make 4 or 5 indentations in the top of the tomato mixture. Drop one uncooked egg into each. Sprinkle the top with the cheese. Cover and cook over medium-low heat about 5 minutes, or until eggs are desired doneness.

Toast the English muffins. Carefully spoon a cooked egg on each muffin half. Spoon remaining sauce over all.

Sausage-Macaroni Quiche

MAKES 6 SERVINGS

A surprisingly easy, delicious main dish to feature at your next Sunday brunch. Serve with a fresh fruit salad.

8 ounces uncooked small macaroni or small shells (about 2 cups)

3 eggs, slightly beaten

2 cups milk

4 ounces smoked sausage links, cut into bite-size pieces

2 green onions, chopped

¼ teaspoon salt

⅛ teaspoon freshly ground black pepper

2 tomatoes, peeled and sliced

2 cups (8 ounces) shredded Cheddar cheese

¼ cup seasoned dried bread crumbs

Cook the pasta according to package directions; drain and set aside.

Preheat oven to 325F (165C). Grease an 11-inch ceramic quiche pan or a 13 × 9-inch baking dish.

While the pasta cooks, combine the eggs, milk, sausage, onions, salt, and pepper in a large bowl. Arrange the cooked pasta in the bottom of prepared pan. Spoon the egg mixture over the pasta. Arrange the tomatoes on top. Toss the cheese with bread crumbs. Sprinkle over top.

Bake the quiche, uncovered, 45 to 55 minutes, or until firm. Cut into wedges or rectangles. Serve hot.

Pizza Brunch Special

MAKES ABOUT 6 SERVINGS

A star performer, this will impress your family and friends at your next brunch.

1 unbaked refrigerated 9-inch piecrust

8 ounces bulk pork sausage

5 eggs, slightly beaten

3 tablespoons milk

¼ teaspoon salt

⅛ teaspoon freshly ground black pepper

½ cup sliced ripe olives

2 tablespoons sliced green onions

10 to 12 cherry tomatoes, halved

1 cup (4 ounces) shredded mozzarella cheese

Preheat oven to 425F (220C). Roll or pat the piecrust into a 13-inch round. Press into a 12-inch pizza pan. Fold over the edges and flute. Prick the bottom with a fork. Bake 12 to 14 minutes, or until light brown.

While the crust bakes, crumble the sausage into a hot 8-inch skillet. Cook until brown, stirring to break up. Remove the sausage with a slotted spoon; drain off all except 1 tablespoon of the drippings from skillet. Set the sausage aside.

Beat the eggs, milk, salt, and pepper in a large bowl. Pour into drippings in skillet. Cook, stirring, until firm. Spoon scrambled eggs onto baked pastry. Top with the sausage, olives, onions, and tomatoes. Sprinkle cheese over all.

Return pizza to oven; bake about 5 minutes, or until cheese melts. Cut into wedges.

VARIATION

The cooked filling can be combined with the toppings and rolled up in warm flour tortillas to make breakfast burritos. Serve with salsa.

Chili Pizza

MAKES 4 SERVINGS

Frozen bread dough thaws in 1 to 2 hours at room temperature or 6 to 8 hours in the refrigerator.

1 (1-pound) loaf frozen bread dough

2 tablespoons vegetable oil

1 (15-oz.) can chili without beans

3 small plum tomatoes, thinly sliced

1 small green bell pepper, diced

3 small green onions, including tops, thinly sliced

1 cup (4 ounces) shredded Cheddar cheese

1 cup (4 ounces) shredded mozzarella cheese

1 teaspoon dried oregano, crushed

Brush the frozen bread dough with oil; thaw according to package directions.

Preheat oven to 425F (220C). Lightly grease a 12-inch pizza pan. With fingers, pat the thawed dough out to a 12-inch round on the prepared pan.

Spread the chili over the dough to within ½ inch of the edge. Top with the tomato slices, bell pepper, and onions. Combine the cheeses and sprinkle evenly over top. Sprinkle with the oregano.

Bake 20 minutes, or until brown and bubbly. Cut into 8 wedges.

Zucchini Sausage Pizza

MAKES 6 SERVINGS

A delicious layer of shredded zucchini replaces the traditional pizza crust. Hot Italian sausage adds a nice spiciness.

1 teaspoon olive oil

8 ounces hot Italian sausage links

1 (8-oz.) can tomato sauce

1 teaspoon dried Italian seasoning, crushed

4 cups lightly packed shredded zucchini (about 2 pounds)

½ cup finely chopped onion

2 tablespoons minced fresh parsley

8 tablespoons fine dried bread crumbs

2 cups (8 ounces) shredded mozzarella cheese

1 egg, beaten

½ teaspoon salt

¼ teaspoon freshly ground black pepper

⅓ cup freshly grated Parmesan cheese

Heat the olive oil in a 9-inch skillet over medium-high heat. Remove the casings from the sausage links; crumble into skillet. Cook until lightly browned, stirring to break up. Add the tomato sauce and Italian seasoning; remove from heat and set aside.

Preheat oven to 350F (175C). Combine the zucchini, onion, parsley, 6 tablespoons of the bread crumbs, 1 cup of the mozzarella cheese, the egg, salt, and pepper in a medium bowl; mix well.

Lightly grease a 12-inch pizza pan; sprinkle with the remaining 2 tablespoons of bread crumbs. Using a spoon, pat the zucchini mixture into pizza pan. Sprinkle the remaining mozzarella cheese over the zucchini mixture. Spoon the tomato-meat mixture evenly over the mozzarella cheese, covering as much as possible. Sprinkle with the Parmesan cheese.

Bake 30 to 35 minutes, or until golden. Let stand 5 to 10 minutes. Cut into wedges and serve warm.

COMPARISON TO METRIC MEASURE

When You Know	Symbol	Multiply By	To Find	Symbol
teaspoons	tsp.	5.0	milliliters	ml
tablespoons	tbsp.	15.0	milliliters	ml
fluid ounces	fl. oz.	30.0	milliliters	ml
cups	c	0.24	liters	l
pints	pt.	0.47	liters	l
quarts	qt.	0.95	liters	l
ounces	oz.	28.0	grams	g
pounds	lb.	0.45	kilograms	kg
Fahrenheit	F	5/9 (after subtracting 32)	Celsius	C

FAHRENHEIT TO CELSIUS

F	C
200–205	95
220–225	105
245–250	120
275	135
300–305	150
325–330	165
345–350	175
370–375	190
400–405	205
425–430	220
445–450	230
470–475	245
500	260

LIQUID MEASURE TO MILLILITERS

1/4 teaspoon	=	1.25	milliliters
1/2 teaspoon	=	2.5	milliliters
3/4 teaspoon	=	3.75	milliliters
1 teaspoon	=	5.0	milliliters
1-1/4 teaspoons	=	6.25	milliliters
1-1/2 teaspoons	=	7.5	milliliters
1-3/4 teaspoons	=	8.75	milliliters
2 teaspoons	=	10.0	milliliters
1 tablespoon	=	15.0	milliliters
2 tablespoons	=	30.0	milliliters

LIQUID MEASURE TO LITERS

1/4 cup	=	0.06 liters
1/2 cup	=	0.12 liters
3/4 cup	=	0.18 liters
1 cup	=	0.24 liters
1-1/4 cups	=	0.3 liters
1-1/2 cups	=	0.36 liters
2 cups	=	0.48 liters
2-1/2 cups	=	0.6 liters
3 cups	=	0.72 liters
3-1/2 cups	=	0.84 liters
4 cups	=	0.96 liters
4-1/2 cups	=	1.08 liters
5 cups	=	1.2 liters
5-1/2 cups	=	1.32 liters

Index

Mable Hoffman

Mable Hoffman is a professional home economist and director of Hoffman Food Consultants. She concentrates her efforts on food consulting, food styling, recipe development, and writing.

Included in Mable's writings are *Mable Hoffman's Crockery Cookery, Healthy Crockery Cookery, Appetizers and Small Meals,* and *Mable and Gar Hoffman's California Flavors.* Her books have won four R. T. French Tastemaker Awards, the "Oscar" for cookbooks, as Best Soft-Cover Cookbook of the year. Both *Crockery Cookery* and *Crepe Cookery* became #1 *New York Times* bestsellers.